Ready?...Time for a change?

Fire!...Use this book!

Aim...Armed with science, real world examples, and a deep understanding of the complex emotional web that defines us as individuals, INSIDE CHANGE is a mandatory 'People 101' course for all innovators, leaders, change agents, and everyone working to transform the future.

– Leigh Anne Cappello, Vice President, Future Now, Hasbro, Inc.

Finally, a book that integrates the basic human function of emotions into a viable action plan for organizational transformation! Its innovative step-by-step guide combines emotional intelligence and organizational change techniques providing leaders with an effective tool that will assist them in competing in a rapid-change global environment. INSIDE CHANGE should be required reading for leaders at all levels of an organization.

– Dr. Thomas G. Seiler, JD, CPA, Professor of Accounting, College of Business, Franklin University

INSIDE CHANGE is a solid, powerful book for every leader. The typical business approach to change just doesn't work – this book will show you a better way.

– Alan Deutschman, author of *Change or Die* and *Walk the Walk*

INSIDE CHANGE provides a powerful and whole-minded approach to organizational transformation. Blending cutting-edge neuroscience with rock-solid business logic, this book will change the way you lead.

– Daniel H. Pink, author of *A Whole New Mind* and *DRIVE*

If your business needs to go from discussing change to executing change this is a must read. Inside Change will be your roadmap for results.

– Jeff Kinsley, HR Manager, FedEx LAC

An excellent book that will help you understand the 'magic' of leadership; managing your EQ to facilitate positive change in organizations that would bring people along.

– Nehad Tadros, Regional HR and Training Manager-GCC, ARAMEX (UAE)

It's a pleasure and an honour to me to present this book that at last approaches in a complementary way "the two half of the sky". In fact, it is not possible to face a change without considering logic and rationality, but not even, at the same time, the emotional aspects of it.

– Luigi Boaretto, Chemical Company, Italy

Inside Change:

Transforming Your Organization with Emotional Intelligence

Joshua Freedman & Massimiliano Ghini, MBA

Foreword by Chip Conley

INSIDE CHANGE:
Transforming Your Organization with Emotional Intelligence

Cover Design by Mark Lee, Incite Partners

ISBN : 978-1-935667-03-2

Library of Congress Control Number: 2010905212

Printed and bound in the United States

Six Seconds Emotional Intelligence Press

San Francisco, California

www.6seconds.org/tools

Contents

Good leaders make people feel that they're at the very heart of things, not at the periphery. Everyone feels that he or she makes a difference to the success of the organization. When that happens people feel centered and that gives their work meaning.

– Warren Bennis

Foreword

Chip Conley, Founder and CEO of the award winning Joie de Vivre Hospitality, California's largest boutique hotel group, and author, PEAK: How Great Companies Get Their Mojo from Maslow *as well as* The Rebel Rules: Daring to be Yourself in Business, *and coauthor of* Marketing That Matters: 10 Practices That Can Profit Your Business and Change the World.

Change is challenging for numerous reasons, but with the right tools, it works.

The first challenge is to remember that organizations are just collections of individuals, and as individuals, we struggle with change. Change provokes a whole range of emotions, and it takes an emotional drive to move us forward. The two most powerful motivations in life that push and pull people to change are fear and love, and there is a place for both. One of the reasons *Inside Change* is so powerful is this recognition: Companies change when people change, and people change through emotion.

The second challenge is expectation. Change is especially challenging when we're already successful. When your past approach has worked for you, why would you change? It's easy to get lulled into a false sense of security. We, as humans, are expectations machines. We build a view of the world based upon how we expect it to be, and how we expect it to be is quite often how it has always been. When reality changes that, we get disappointed.

Here's an "emotional equation" for this reaction: $D = E - R$ (disappointment equals expectations minus reality). When we're confronted by reality that's less than our expectations, we go into a downward spiral of disappointment and frustration that can leave us even more stuck. Later in the book, you'll find more about these "rules" of emotions; the neuroscience in chapter three provides a solid foundation for understanding, and then in chapter seven you'll find new tools to address this challenge.

The third challenge is structure. We build "status quo" into our organizational structures. The org chart reinforces a certain set of expectations created around how things have always been done. So, in addition to the human changes in attitudes and habits, transformation requires rethinking basic structures like the org chart, reporting responsibilities and accountability, and compensation.

We need to face reality. The world is dramatically changing; if we're stagnant and try to do it the way we've always done it, we will actually die. We will not adapt, and the survival of the fittest means we'll be buried with the dinosaurs. Confronting this reality creates fear – which can be helpful.

Fear can be helpful to get people to take action quickly. It's not a good long-term motivator, because fear overuses the adrenal glands, and pushes a kind of short-term protection. That's not sustainable. Fear helps us survive, but it's not going to generate real innovation.

So fear can help generate action, but then we need to know how to move out of it to decide where to go. We need to craft a vision of what change could mean, of the opportunity that comes from change. This picture of a brighter world is fueled by love. That inspires me and gets me excited: it gets people to say "I want to be part of that!"

Once I'm committed to the vision, I'm open to living through some of the adaptation and change that might be difficult in order to get to the new vision. So there is a place and value of fear, and there's a place and value for love. We need both in the right place and in the right way.

When people are disappointed, they feel sad and afraid, and that tends to block this sort of forward momentum. The antidote is a vision that engages them in love. But it's not a magic wand. When people are in that fearful sad place you don't just say a few words and have them move. It's a process to get there and that process depends on the nature of the culture of the organization.

In other words, a vision *statement* is useless. You can pay a fancy marketing firm to come up with beautiful words to put on the wall, and it does nothing (or even makes it worse). We need to go beyond the "vision statement" to consider a "vision process."

The purpose of the vision is to galvanize people to move together toward new possibility. So people need to be part of that process. In Part II, *Inside Change* offers a framework for this process and steps that will allow you to bring people along.

It's a truism at all levels of the organization: when someone feels like they were involved with the process of making a decision they're more committed to the decision. When it's imposed upon them, or when it's some "answer from above," they won't be fully committed.

So, vision requires a company wide conversation. In 2002, during the dot-com bust when things were really a mess in the Bay Area hotel business, we started creating "service retreats." We took all of our employees at the hotel off site for a day (we had staff from one of our other hotels oversee the hotel while the hotel staff was offsite). Housekeepers, bartenders, bellhops would meet with managers, and talk about where we were going in the next year.

Frankly, there was a lot of fear and that time, and some people said we couldn't "afford" this kind of time for reflection. But the process of moving from fear to engagement requires listening to people and hearing how they see their job. Together we could ask, "What is it that our customers are looking for that we currently are not delivering on?"

So instead of presenting some beautiful vision statement, we had a process of coming to vision. Instead of words on the wall, together we created **a** way of living, a way of being that sits in someone's heart.

This process begins with strong, trust-based relationships. I'm a big fan of Abraham Maslow who described these processes with pyramids. We reinterpreted Maslow's five-level Hierarchy of Needs pyramid into three levels.

Trust is the foundation of the relationship, the base that the pyramid is built on, and it creates safety and strength required for survival.

That's true in relationships between employers and employees, between companies and customers and between entrepreneurs and investors.

You create it through transparency and authenticity in communications, through shared understanding of what you've done and why. It comes from an alignment of goals and processes. Perhaps most importantly in organizations, it comes from walking the walk. Leaders are role models, and how you behave, in time, will influence how the company behaves. The last chapter of this book is a powerful reminder of this: If we're going to call ourselves leaders, we need to be worthy of following.

So the first level is a foundation that creates safety. The next level of the pyramid is going from survival to successful performance. It's about executing in a way that's effective and successful, where all parties experience that their actions are visible contributions. The challenge is to ensure that the inputs are executed in a way such that the outputs are creating success.

At the top of the pyramid is transformation. Transformation goes beyond the tangible result to the intangible impact. It creates inspiration in employees, evangelism in customers and that pride of ownership in investors. It's a feeling that, "not only did we succeed, but we made a major difference."

I'm not saying exclusively social responsibility here, although that is certainly a positive way of making a difference in the world. When this is done right, we create a sense of community for everyone involved. We feel connected to these people because together we've gone through something and done something important – we're committed to one another. It's a relationship that transcends the transaction.

The goal is to serve a higher need. A customer might not know what they wanted it, but they walk out changed by the experience and amazed that the company "mind-read" what they truly needed. In the case of the investor, this will touch on that sense of pride of ownership, "yes I made money, but it's way beyond that: it actually made me feel like we made a difference." A transformative investor is one who puts his or her money where their heart is.

This part of the pyramid is a constant thread in the *Inside Change* model: Engage, Activate, Reflect. In the Engage phase, you'll be asked to clarify this purpose and ensure your changes align with it. In the Activate phase, you step toward that purpose by putting it in action in a micro way. Then in Reflect, you use purpose as the benchmark. The goal is to more deeply embed your transformational purpose in the change and in the organization – to bake it in.

At Joie de Vivre, the transformational purpose is built right into our name: Joy of Life. Our mantra is create joy. Our mission statement is creating opportunities to celebrate the joy of life. And we measure it. We measure it for our employees. We measure it for our customers. And it gives us an incredible competitive advantage.

The transformational purpose is essential for making real change because it fuels internal motivation. In those times people feel stuck, when they're in the disappointment, when they're uncertain, they need some inner drive to get past that.

So the base of the pyramid makes it possible to take the risks together. The middle creates performance. And the top provides the fuel to go there. As you'll see later in the book, the three phases of the Inside Change process, Engage, Activate, and Reflect, provide a powerful process for building this kind of rock-solid pyramid in your organization, and in your life.

Chip Conley

San Francisco, April 2010

Introduction

We are privileged to do wonderful work. Perhaps the greatest excitement is seeing individuals, teams, and organizations succeed at change. They come to us in a place of struggle and uncertainty, usually having tried many times to successfully transform. Then together, usually, we're able to make something new happen.

In the last decade working with a wide variety of clients, from multinationals to family businesses to government agencies to schools to individual people, we've learned a few important lessons about change that we hope to share with you.

The most important lesson is that **change begins on the inside.**

We decided to write this book because so many of our clients and colleagues struggle with change. Nearly everyone we talk to is inundated with change. They tell us that they are making good plans, but the plans are not fully working. We hope that this book will provide an important part of the solution – and as a result, our organizations and communities around the world will be better, and do better for and with their people.

Thank you for reading, and we look forward to hearing from you about the book. Please visit the book's Web site to reach us, and for more resources: www.insidechange.net

Joshua Freedman, San Francisco

Massimiliano Ghini, Bologna

Part I

Background

The change model and processes that we'll share in this book grew from three important sources:

1. The real challenges that colleagues and clients face when making change are primarily on the people-side. In Chapter 1, we'll present a summary and the "case" for the need to improve the way business approaches change.

2. The process that has worked in addressing these issues. In Chapter 2, we'll show you the components of the Change MAP.

3. Current neuroscience that provides critical new perspectives to understand people and change. In Chapter 3, we'll review this science and make it relevant to the challenges of change.

Growth demands

a temporary surrender

of security.

– Gail Sheehy

Chapter 1. The Problem

What do you think of when you hear CHANGE? Excitement? Anxiety? Frustration? Exhaustion? Almost certainly you have some feelings about this loaded topic, and even people who thrive on change acknowledge that it's incredibly challenging. And it's accelerating.

Organizationally, navigating change is a growing issue. The percentage of CEOs expecting substantial change is higher than ever; 65 percent in 2006 to 83 percent in 2008.[1] While the need is growing, the rate of success is not keeping up.

In 1996, John Kotter published his best seller *Leading Change* and stated that 70% of change efforts fail. Now over a decade later, despite hundreds of "change breakthroughs" shared in books and conference talks, the percentage of failure remains about the same. In a 2008 McKinsey survey of thousands, people reported that 2/3 of change efforts failed. In IBM's 2009 "Making change work" study of more than 1500 change leaders worldwide, IBM found that 60% of change efforts failed.

Clearly change is not an easy process. Why? What makes it so difficult? And how do real managers see these issues?

We invited leaders to identify the key challenges in the workplace today in Six Seconds' ongoing Workplace Issues survey. The research explores perceptions of people in organizations, from team leaders to executives in a broad range of industries, and entities ranging from under 20 to over 10,000 people.

The survey finds that…

- "Soft" issues such as change and leadership are 3 times as prevalent as "hard" issues such as finance.

- 50% of Leaders are concerned about managing change.

- Emotional dynamics of team- and non-team-members

- were the most important challenge.

- Only 8% report that they've received training to effectively deal with the issues they're facing.[2]

This last point is staggering. In the US alone, in ONE year, companies spend US$130 billion on learning and development,[3] but less than one in ten respondents in our survey is getting the training they need to deal with the issues they're facing today? Something is missing.

To explore this further, last year we asked dozens of groups of managers around the world to identify the most important methods needed for their organizations to be more effective at change; we gave them 10 minutes to brainstorm. Group after group came up with a set of very reasonable answers, including:

- Create urgency

- Get people committed

- Make a clear plan

- Make the results visible

- Get quick wins

It's a great start. What we've seen in groups over and over is that today managers know a lot about change. But at the same time, 60-70% of change efforts are failing. Something is wrong! Digging deeper, what we've heard is:

✓ Managers know WHAT to do in change, they don't know HOW.

They are clear that there are certain key steps, but getting themselves and others committed to those steps is the heart of the challenge.

Meanwhile the pace is increasing. Around 1940, Eric Johnson, president of the US Chamber of Commerce, issued a shocking proclamation: "knowledge is doubling every ten years."[4] Then came the internet. By 2004, we were down to information doubling every 18 months.[5] IBM Global Technology Services predicts that by now information is doubling every 11 hours, with business email growing at a rate of 25-30% annually.[6] Complexity is increasing at an accelerating rate, but our capacity for change is not. No wonder change is such a pressing issue!

It seems that there is a widespread understanding of the need but lack of answers on how to meet it. We know change is important, we know people issues are important. Meanwhile we keep doing the same old processes and training people the same old ways, probably because we don't see real alternatives. This is a serious warning for companies.

✓ We are living extraordinary times but we're stuck using ordinary answers.

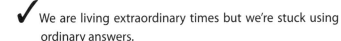

We are creating an increasingly complex and accelerating world and we don't know how to manage it – unless 30-40% success is satisfactory. In other words, even when leaders understand the right thing to do, it's unlikely those efforts will work because of execution problems. Considering how much money, people power, technology and time we are putting in change management efforts, it seems like we might want to re-allocate our investments!

Obstacles to Change

Clearly it's time to re-think the problem. Why are we **still** struggling with change?   Is it an innate human problem?   There's plenty of evidence that change is possible; in fact, humans are actually marvelous at change. [7] But we get stuck. What are the traps?

We began our exploration for this book with an extensive search of "thought leadership" on change, and found three common assumptions that may be at the heart of the problem:

Summary:

P. 17

1. Change is linear – change starts, ends, and is complete.

2. Leave emotions at the door – change is primarily a cognitive process.

3. Organizational change is driven by system change – change starts with structures, policies, models, etc.

It's our view that these assumptions are tragically flawed, and that by seriously re-evaluating these ideas, we can arrive at a dramatically more effective approach to change. In exploring these three common misassumptions, you'll see the thinking that underlies the Change MAP and the solution we'll share later in the book.

Misassumption 1. Change is linear

Once upon a time, perhaps, change occurred "once in a while" to tune up operations; today change is the norm. It's amusing to talk to clients about the strings of mergers and acquisitions they've experienced in the last few years. A typical story: "I've been through 5 M&As in four years – and I'm still doing the same job at the same desk for the same clients."

The notion of "a change" just doesn't fit this reality. We need to focus on "changing" or "changeability" – a constant process of learning, innovation, and adaptability. Not only is each organization constantly in change, at the same time the context is in flux – globalization, climate, regulation, economic meltdown, generation gaps, increased transparency... If we could only perfect the crystal ball we'd have a great market! Until then, even knowing the right direction a day ahead is a real challenge. So, we have a chaotic, uncertain environment that's going fast – and faster. The old view of a linear change just won't work. We need a cycle that can be rapidly deployed to create a system of continuous growth and adaptability.

The conventional, linear, approach to change is to get ready, aim, and then fire. This is great in theory and terrible in practice. In the "ready-aim-fire" approach, planners (perhaps a project team and a few expensive consultants) create a roadmap and senior managers allocate resources to make a plan. Then, they "aim" - spending weeks and months developing a "great" strategy, usually accompanied by hundreds of powerpoint slides and a massive excel workbook. When it comes time to "fire" - implement - everyone is surprised that the "perfect plan" doesn't work immediately, so they throw that out, hire new consultants and start writing a new one. And likely, the new plan will be made in a vacuum, be out-of-date by the time it launches, and then use so much resource in planning that there's nothing left for follow-through.

Ready, Aim, Fire is a linear process that blocks change-ability.

How to Solve This Misassumption

The common explanation is that "people resist change." That's sometimes true, but our experience is that people are more likely to resist a bad process than the change itself. They might actually like change, but don't like "being changed." The fact is people thrive on change, people are incredibly versatile and nimble, they change all their lives over and over, and growth is one of the most stimulating and enriching opportunities in the human experience. So we're not talking about making dinosaurs do the polka. It's not an impossible situation – rather, we need to underline the importance of structuring the change.

✔ We need a way to conceptualize change as a living process with built-in mechanisms for continuous refinement.

In the "ready-aim-fire" framework, projects tend to sit in "ready-aim" and rarely get to "fire." Frustration builds, then a senior exec comes in waving a hatchet to make change happen and there's "fire" "fire" "fire" – without much aim. Clearly all three would be valuable – ready, aim, fire – but perhaps the order is wrong.

Misassumption 2. Leave emotions at the door
....

We often hear leaders say, in essence, "People will change when they understand this is better for the company and better for them." The basic belief is that a clear, logical business case will create change. Change managers are often engineers trained to break the complex down into a rational structure. That would work well if people were rational. But people are not, purely, rational... especially in change!

How do **you** feel when you hear the word "change"? It's a question we regularly ask clients. Some react with optimism and excitement while others feel anger or fear.

We recently did a keynote for 1000 future leaders and asked: How many of you are excited when you hear the word "change?" **One** person raised his hand. Maybe that's extreme, but it's telling. The bottom line: people have strong feelings about change.

 CHANGE is not a neutral word!

Part of the problem with conventional change efforts is that they come on the heels of many other similar efforts – and most of those have fallen short. So people "know" this new change won't work. Even when there is a logical plan, even when there's a beautiful powerpoint outlining the path forward, people's trust in change has been eroded. So change leaders need to use emotional intelligence to connect at a heart-level (and they need the strategic intelligence to connect at a head-level too).

One of our clients was going through a complex restructuring process and was meeting with one of the world's largest consulting firms. The consultant showed this slide to underline the importance of the emotional dynamics in change process. His message: if you want to have success in a change you need to manage the emotional side of the business.

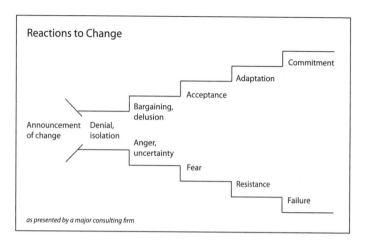

as presented by a major consulting firm

Impressed and surprised, our client said: "Great! Finally we're discussing the core issue. So how can we transform resistance in adaptation? How do we make sure we stay on that 'commitment' path?"

The consultant's profound answer: "That's the magic of leadership."

Imagine our surprise to discover that you have to be magical to be a great leader! In essence, the consultant was saying, "I don't know." Which is a pity because he put his finger on an absolutely critical point. The fact is that "downward path" toward resistance and rejection is the biggest risk in any change process, this destructive spiral erodes performance and makes future change even more difficult – and it's all about emotion.

There is a great deal written about the cognitive side of change – how to think through change, how to analyze change, how to strategically position change efforts. No question that is important, but it's incomplete, because change is not simply a cognitive experience. It would be easier if people were rational; "it's better for you to exercise," ZAP people would exercise! "We can increase performance by implementing LEAN in one quarter," ZAM there'd be a full LEAN process in place. But people are not only rational, so we need to understand the impact of emotions in the process.

Are emotions a killer app in managing change? The research is emerging; for example, one study of 615 people in government and private companies affected by huge organizational changes in Australia: 44% of the resistance to change is explained by emotions and assumptions.[8]

In another study, a variety of change-drivers were analyzed including reward, job satisfaction, participation, history of change, etc., to see what contributes to commitment to change. By far the strongest predictor is emotional involvement ($r=.423$), the next strongest is a history of successful change ($r=.267$). So emotional involvement is almost twice as strong a predictor as any other factor – even having previously succeeded. Reward wasn't even statistically significant.[9]

How to Solve This Misassumption

The key is to be more intelligent with emotions. Emotional intelligence provides the capacity to accurately see and understand these feeling dynamics, and then to create effective solutions.

The value of emotional intelligence in people-performance is evident in many studies;[10] one example is research we conducted in healthcare which showed that people with higher emotional intelligence cope better with job complexity and with stress in the workplace, two issues that often arise with change – and the effect was greater in more senior roles.[11]

On the lighter side, one powerful emotional tool is humor. An interesting study by Bovey and Hede shows that people who use humor to cope with anxiety have less resistance to organi-

Emotions & Stress in Healthcare

As in many demanding jobs, health care is stressful work with high-stakes challenges, a fast pace, and complex relationships. In the face of these pressures, professionals must carefully manage their reactions and interactions to achieve optimal outcomes. How important is emotional intelligence (EQ) for managing these dynamics? How does EQ affect stress and performance?

To test this, two assessments were administered:

SEI – Six Seconds Emotional Intelligence Assessment.

SPA - Stress Perception Audit

The study finds three important conclusions:

- Emotional intelligence predicts high performance

- Stress reduces performance

- Emotional intelligence mitigates the effects of stress.

A reasonable inference emerges that one of the primary benefits of high EQ is the increased ability to function well even under stress.

Interestingly, the most senior group in the study – those with the most supervisory and leadership responsibilities – are the ones where emotional intelligence made the most difference. This finding suggests that in increasingly complex jobs, EQ becomes increasingly important.[11]

zational change.[12]

It's even more evident in personal changes. Ask anyone who has tried and failed at dieting. Being healthy is really simple: Eat less, exercise and sleep more, drink water. Rocket science, right? Everyone who's tried to lose weight KNOWS this – but many of us struggle for years to do it. As Bruce Lee said:

> Knowing is not enough, you must apply; willing is not enough, you must do.

But what does it take to go from knowledge to action? Emotion is the missing link – at home and at work, it's the critical ingredient to propel people into doing.

 Emotions drive people, people drive performance!

One of the key emotional drivers in change is trust; it's like a speed governor that limits (or unlocks) action. When she tells you that we need to change, do you trust your boss? Robert Hurley recently surveyed 450 executives in 30 companies from around the world and his findings are worrisome: **half of all managers don't trust their leaders**.[13] Hurley also reported another survey from Golin Harris showing 69% of respondents agreed with the statement "I just don't know who to trust anymore." Yet trust is crucial if we want people to "come along with us" on the change journey, so this balance has to shift (or at least we'd better make sure our team members are in the 31% who know who to trust!).

Taking trust as a benchmark, the "emotional currency," if you will, we need leaders who use authenticity rather than flash. An example is the incredible turnaround of IBM in the 1990s. As Lou Gerstner, the CEO in charge for the change, described in his book, *Who Says Elephants Can't Dance?*, the real problem was that team members had lost faith in the company. Gerstner saw his responsibility was to inspire people about the opportunity to be a great company again.

Put yourself in Gerstner's shoes for a moment. Clearly reinvigorating "Big Blue" won't succeed by simply rewriting the mission statement and moving the same old boxes on an org chart. You would need to create a massive emotional transition to create a new culture. To realize this shift people need to sense your commitment and feel your authentic passion. They need to trust you. And that's all about emotions!

It's also worth noting that Gerstner came to the job as a "typical MBA engineer" type with no particular gift at rhetoric. He wasn't a "heroic" leader. While the old-style charismatic leader can give a great locker-room speech and fire people up, this relationship-based change leadership requires a more subtle process. When people are coming from hopelessness and distrust, their radar is up. Again, they "know" that the change won't work. They don't trust the system, so they're actively looking for another snow job. Authenticity beats slick.

Finally, while sincerity is key, the emotional component is not sufficient by itself. Change will be derailed by a lack of buy-in, but it is equally useless to launch change without a good plan. We're not advocating that "heart over head" replace the worn-out "head over heart" mindset, rather we're calling for a partnership of head+heart+hands.

Misassumption 3. Organizational change is driven by changing systems

We were delivering training to a group of senior MBA professors in a highly regarded university, and gave them a challenging exercise where they had 10 minutes to plan, and then couldn't

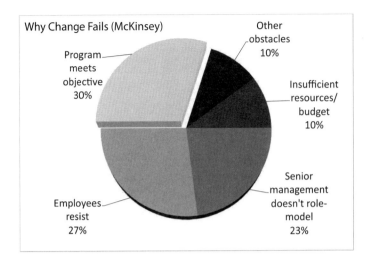

talk during the implementation (though they could communicate nonverbally). They made a "great" plan, but did a miserable job on the challenge. In the debriefing, we asked what went wrong: "We had an excellent strategy, but there was an execution problem." We pressed back: "Was it really a great strategy if you couldn't follow it?" They were adamant that the strategy was optimal despite the failure.

In the same way, organizational change projects are usually planned and structured at a systemic level only to break down at the human level. In their seminal research about change, McKinsey found that the real problem is on the people side: 50% of change failure lies in resistance to change and a lack of example from the senior managers. In other words, changing an organization is not about writing a new organizational chart or redefining the mission statement; it's about facilitating people to change.

IBM developed similar findings: change fails primarily due to people issues. Over 60% of change leaders identify the real issue as how to change people's behavior, and 49% think the real problem is to be capable of changing the organizational culture.

A strategy is only powerful if it can and will be implemented by the people who are responsible for execution.

How to Solve This Misassumption

Strategy needs to begin and end with people.

This is the reason why Jeff Immelt, CEO of General Electric, is working hard to create a new culture of change in GE. In a recent interview in Harvard Business Review he said: my job is to "drive change and develop others as leaders." To do that he created a change program called LIG (Leadership, Innovation and Growth) where for the first time all the senior members of a business's management team were trained together. The results were great; revenues from internal growth increased 9% in 2007, surpassing Immelt's goal for the third year. The question is: what's made the difference? The course permitted managers to create a shared vocabulary and knowledge about the barriers to change, work on how people change, and then define a concrete action plan to change. He created engagement in the management team.

Immelt concluded the interview saying, "I still have to push, and I think that will always be true. But there are now more people pushing with me." This is a crucial part of change – when a person is going one way, and has had years of learning a particular approach, it's a big effort to redirect that. Think of it as a physics problem; to change the direction of a vector, you have to apply a new force. Multiply by 10 for a team, and by a thousand or more for a whole organization. Difficult change requires massive effort – which will only come from growing a committed group.

So, we have three misassumptions, and three antidotes:

Misassumption	Problem	Antidote
Change is linear	We are not dealing with one simple change	Create a dynamic process for ongoing changeability
Leave emotions at the door	Humans are not only rational	Become effective with the emotional side
Organizational change will occur by changing systems	Strategies don't work if people won't or can't execute them	Put people at the center of the planning

At the core, the problem of change is a human problem. So, if we want to really change an organization, we need to understand how people change. But first let's consider: Is change even possible?

Can People Change?

When the stakes are high, life and death for the people or the company, change will happen – right? *Fast Company* senior writer Alan Deutschman was surprised that the answer is "no." He was attending a conference on the future of healthcare where the Dean of Johns Hopkins Medical School talked about what happens to cardiac patients when they're told to "change or die." The incident led to an in-depth analysis of individual and organizational change with a startling conclusion: While change is possible, the usual approach doesn't work.

When the doctor stands up in the authority of his lab coat, shakes his finger at you, and tells you all the reasons that you have to change or die, he's relying on a particular paradigm, a tragically flawed "conventional wisdom" that people will change through the Three Fs: Force, Facts, and Fear.

One reason the Force, Facts, and Fear, FFF-driven change fails is the inattention to a basic principle of emotional intelligence: **When people feel pushed, they resist.** When facts and fear are used to try and force change, people may comply in the short term, but they don't have a real ownership of the change. It's obedience, not motivation. In the Six Seconds Emotional Intelligence Model, this concept is captured in the competency of Intrinsic Motivation. Without Intrinsic Motivation, people will not persevere, even if something is "good for them." So an effective change leader will go beyond logic to engage people at a heart level.

 The best news is that change is possible. It just takes a different approach.

Extensive research has shown that the most successful change actually begins with an emotionally significant relationship. In the 1950s, psychologists at Johns Hopkins University began to study what forms of psychotherapy worked, and hundreds of studies have followed up on this work. The surprising conclusion: They all work equally well, or equally poorly – the system isn't the determining factor. Successful change is determined by the relationship; a relationship that creates hope.[14] The feeling of hope is essential, and it comes partly from the logical side – seeing results – and largely from something less tangible.

When "everything's perfect," few people focus on change. Usually change gets a lot of attention when things are falling apart. The worse the situation, the more urgently people seek change, and the worse it gets, the less hopeful people become. This pessimism is a natural consequence of the ongoing churn in corporate life – the annual (or sometimes quarterly) "transformational strategy" unleashed by some well-meaning and well-paid consulting firm. You can just hear the middle managers' "here we go again" refrain as the latest in an incessant string of changes come rolling over them, doomed before it starts by a lack of buy-in.

The antidote isn't a more logical plan, it's a more compelling relationship. What we need is a leader who can give us a hope for change. This emotional need goes far beyond a paycheck. Yes, people need to pay the bills, but they also need something deeper, and some leaders have committed to provide that.

Deutschman offers an example from the 1990s when General Motors closed a plant because the workers were "unmanageable." The old paradigm was "telling people to do something and relying on the force of threatening to fire them if they didn't." When Toyota took over the plant, they tried a different set of motivators. "They took these American workers to Japan and showed them how this actually worked on the assembly lines in Japan. You can't just tell people something. You have to prove it to them through experience. They set up a situation appealing to people's desire to be competent, to be creative, to be successful, and to be admired and respected for those skills by the people they work with." *Best practices.*

Like many others, Deutschman concludes that people are, in fact, great at change. People love learning, are curious, innovative and adaptable. Just look at how much people learn – a 90-year-old can get herself on Facebook, a six-year-old can create a Lego space cruiser. The process of learning offers several key tips for change.

David Kolb's research suggested that learning is a process where you need to understand information, absorb it, practice it and integrate it with the existing knowledge. In others words, you have to give time to learners to reflect, experiment and apply the new knowledge. So a powerful change model should mirror that:

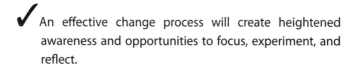 An effective change process will create heightened awareness and opportunities to focus, experiment, and reflect.

Chris Argyris adds that your learning will be boosted if you have to teach what you learned. Teaching back creates a deeper level of ownership and pushes the learner to make sense of the new data in a personal way. So:

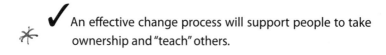 An effective change process will support people to take ownership and "teach" others.

Because this is such a critical resource of change leaders, we'll share more of the cutting-edge science of learning and the brain in Chapter 3.

Lead or follow.
But don't block.
Naslaa and train the trainers

Recap

While essential for organizational success, change is challenging. Although many approaches to change recognize that these challenges are both strategic and emotional, the usual premise is that a "great strategy" will make people fall into line. This passing regard to the people who must execute the change leads most change efforts to fail. Instead, we need an approach based on understanding the human and emotional drivers of change and engaging those to assist in forming and executing effective strategy.

This view is a natural extension of decades of leading thinking on change. Kurt Lewin, the pioneering social psychologist and author of *Group Decision and Social Change*, recognized that behavior is driven by the interaction of people and their environment. Applying his Force Field Analysis, Lewin identified that successful organizational change begins with "unfreezing," an essential process of both strategic and emotional planning. Then he said, new learning has to occur before "re-freezing" in the changed state. William Bridges, author of *Managing Transition,* advocates for leaders to attend to the emotional transition of change and provides a powerful concept of "transition" that we'll use to understand the emotional dynamics of change. John Kotter, author of *Leading Change*, offers a process for change that begins with the importance of emotional engagement. We'll take that a step further and put people and purpose at the center of the change – so they own and drive change, not just once, but in an expanding cycle of growth.

It is not necessary to change.

Survival is not mandatory.

– W. Edwards Deming

Chapter 2. The Solution

So far we've identified:

- Change is a critical issue.

- While people are highly adaptable, typical processes for change are not very successful.

Based on the misassumptions we explored in Chapter One, a better change process will:

- Be cyclical rather than linear

- Include emotion versus pretending people are purely rational

- Focus on people as the driver of the strategy

So, let's build a new change model in line with these three parameters.

Cyclical

In essence, change is a process of learning – learning a new approach, new systems, new ways of thinking, feeling, and acting. So we'll start with a fairly conventional "action learning"[15] model built for continuous growth, then we'll adapt it into a powerful and totally new framework for change.

In this framework, change (and learning) succeeds when it proceeds through three continuously cycling phases: Engage, Activate, and Reflect.

Engage	READY	put the change in focus
Activate	FIRE	experiment and apply
Reflect	AIM	tune up the process for the next time around

When we present this model, some people have an immediate concern. "Ready-fire-aim," they say, "but that's crazy – you have to aim in order to hit anything!" True enough, and we're not doing away with that phase, just putting it in a more effective position, which we can do because we've turned the linear process into a rapid cycle. This works both in the metaphorical and literal sense.

In terms of the metaphor, think of old war ships. On seeing a threat, they would run out their guns (ready), shoot a "ranging shot" to test their setup (fire), then calibrate closer to the target (aim). They would repeat the cycle over and over yielding more and more accuracy over time.

As we discussed in Chapter 1, the ready-fire-aim approach solves a critical problem in most change efforts. If you take the time to fully aim, the "target" has moved before you get to fire.

It's important to remember this is an iterative, or spiraling, process. As you move through the cycle you gain clarity and accuracy – and momentum.

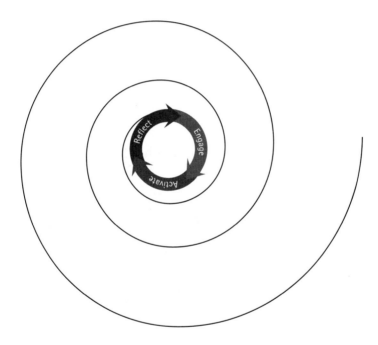

This cyclical approach to change allows for a rapid cycle time creating short-term wins that demonstrate the efficacy. Often change efforts fail because they attempt to skip over or short-change one phase. By keeping the cycle focused and spiraling outward, we increase the likelihood of reaching all three phases even in today's hectic business world.

Rational+Emotional

The action learning cycle is great from a rational viewpoint. We make a plan, experiment-innovate-apply, and refine. But as we discussed earlier, "change is not a neutral subject."

When change is flowing smoothly, that's fabulous, and they don't need you or us to help. When it's stuck, however, watch out! People begin feeling discouraged, their frustration mounts, they get into blame, and they begin to feel fear because they don't know how to get out of the mess, and the feelings escalate.

So, when we're "acting like people" and reacting with these difficult emotions, we go into the cycle of resistance.

As you can see in the graphic, the arrows "spin" the opposite direction from the learning cycle. When people are in resistance, they resist! They block change.

Frustration

Judgment

Fear

When you're pushing for change, you might judge that resistance as bad. You might also get frustrated, judge, and even feel afraid that you won't be able to change this. But it's not **bad** to resist change – it's normal. Even when the change is "good for us" sometimes we resist. It's part of the messy, challenging, fabulous nature of people. We'll talk more about that later in the book, but let's just acknowledge it now. While we are great a reasoning, and while many of us love to figure things out logically, there's another side.

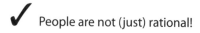 People are not (just) rational!

But that works two ways. Yes, emotions can block change, but they can also FUEL change. If we're smart with feelings, then we can generate feelings that move the cycle forward, like this:

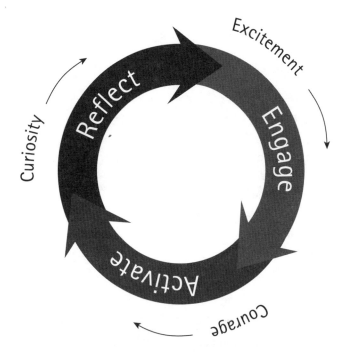

It's pretty easy to see that these kinds of feelings, excitement, courage, and curiosity, form the cycle of engagement. They provide a motive force to "spin" the wheel, and they build on each other. As you move through the phases of change with those feelings, you'll add energy to the wheel generating more of those powerful feelings and accelerating the change process.

The challenge, though, is how to get from the cycle of resistance to the cycle of engagement. Here's a depiction of that shift:

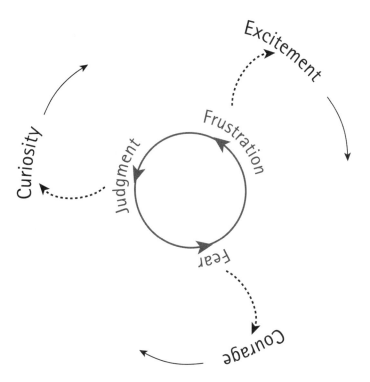

The "dotted arrows" represent a core focus of the emotionally intelligent change leader – you! We call these arrows "transitions," representing the emotional journey that will make or break the change process.

Alchemy of Emotions

The work of the "dotted arrows" is about transition, the emotional work of change. William Bridges introduced a distinction between "Change" and "Transition"; change is the actual move, transition is the psychological process of preparing and following through on the move. Transition is the "process people go through as they internalize and come to terms with the details of the new situation that the change brings about." [16] The core work of the "EQ Change Leader" is to be aware of this emotional dynamic and manage it to optimize the human potential of the process.

Just for example, suppose you are going to shake up a team and reassign people. Probably before the change is even announced, people are beginning to pick up signals and emotions will begin to escalate. Then in the weeks before the change, people will think and feel about what's happening; depending on how that's handled, this will help them prepare, and/or undermine their preparation. Finally the day of the change comes and, at the end of the day, the people are in new offices. Over the next days and weeks, maybe even months, they'll process the experience, adapting to the new reality (perhaps happily, or perhaps pining for their old team). In any case, the transition unfolds over weeks or months, while the actual change took a few hours to plan and a day to execute. The transition is individual and emotional where the change is tactical.

The most critical emotional factor in "crossing the dotted lines" is safety. Change is a risk – it means moving from the known (though often unpleasant, it's still known) to the unknown. So automatically change is loaded with emotional challenge. Add on top that people often experience change as "being done to them," and it's no surprise they feel this resistance. The "cycle of resistance" is a form of protection, the natural response to threat. It's important to recognize that in this case "threat" has little to do with facts.

The mainstream view of the workplace encourages a factual, results-orientated approach that usually minimizes the importance of emotion. Many business leaders come to see everything in their organization as quantifiable, denying (albeit unconsciously) even their own emotions with regard to change. Then, when emotion surfaces, these leaders become frustrated by the "irrational" responses, and attempt to beat emotions into submission with more logic. This may lead to a simple but profound invalidation of people's feelings, which will cause the Cycle of Resistance to spin faster... which pushes the leader to become even more frustrated and deny the emotions (including his own) with even more vigor, which creates even more resistance. The people's initial resistance is often driven underground becoming invisible to the leader, but it's still there. Because the leader no longer perceives this, s/he believes that the problem has been solved. The reality is now it may be more difficult for the people to engage in the desired transitions. In addition, valuable information that comes from openly exploring resistance will be lost.[17]

One of our clients received feedback on their organizational climate assessment that many employees expressed fear of retribution and a perception that the leadership team was not trustworthy. In debriefing this with the leadership team, the dominant reaction was to refute the feedback based on facts. The CFO was indignant: "That's an old story and it's been blown way out of proportion - that kind of retribution just doesn't happen here and we've told people that over and over." What he missed, of course, is that the facts are not the issue; the employees' fear is real, and the feedback is a signal that there's a lack of safety. The CFO's reaction is actually a confirmation of the underlying issue: In essence he was denying people's feelings and telling them they are wrong to feel afraid. Imagine if you didn't trust your boss, but you took a risk to express a fear -- and his response is, "You're wrong so shut up about this!" Would that increase your trust?

In other words, when we're dealing with emotions, facts are not that important. That's very frustrating for people who live in a quantitative mindset, i.e., most businesspeople!

 ✓ Emotions are real, even when they are not based on something real.

To be an emotionally intelligence change leader, the challenge is to manage both the factual and the emotional level, and, perhaps the fundamental emotional dynamic is the balance between fear and trust. Perhaps we could make a "see saw" and consider the weight of two sides:

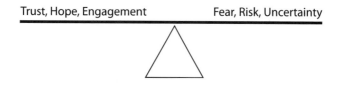

Trust, Hope, Engagement   Fear, Risk, Uncertainty

Trust, hope, and engagement move us toward change, fear and risk move us away. Sometimes people don't use the word "fear" because it's so loaded and, in some organizational cultures, con-notes a kind of weakness (though we've found it to be powerful and courageous when people articulate their fears), so consider some of the other feelings that go with Fear and Trust:

Trust	Fear
Commitment	Doubt
Passion	Concern
Safe	Unsafe
Inclusion	Rejection
Acceptance	Denial
Connection	Distance
Open	Closed
What else?	Add yours!

✔ If you want people to cross the dotted lines, you need enough power in the trust column.

We can now integrate this finding in our model:

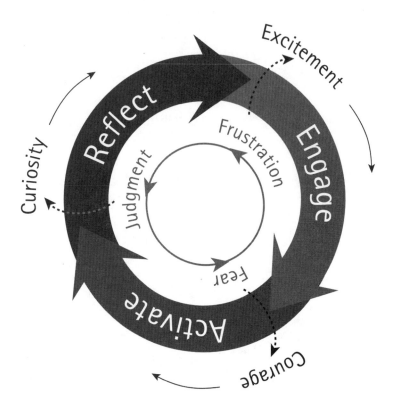

In the next chapter you'll learn more about the way emotion is involved in learning and in group dynamics; we've found that when people understand some of the neuroscience of how emotion and cognition work, it makes it easier for them to first understand, then manage, the transitions. Then, in Part Two, we'll provide important perspective about the emotional transitions in each phase (Engage, Activate, Reflect). Finally, in Part Three, we'll offer additional practical suggestions for working with emotions. That said, if you're not already working to develop emotional intelligence, it's a priority.

People-Driven

It's time to understand: How can we support the people-side of change in the cycle? Every phase of the model has a goal and an emotional transition to manage:

Phase	Goal	Transition
Engage	Buy into a plan	Frustration -> Excitement
Activate	Experience success	Fear -> Courage
Reflect	Lock in wins	Judgment -> Curiosity

Here is the process in brief:

- **Engage**: create buy-in to a plan. This requires a trusting emotional connection with the change leader(s) who encourage hope and build confidence, as well as a careful, effective plan that will produce results.

- **Activate**: experience success. This requires an increase of capability and the opportunity to practice and master new patterns and skills needed to operationalize change and growth.

- **Reflect**: lock in wins. Here change leaders must see and celebrate successes – and foster curiosity to re-imagine the future. On the analytical side, this is the opportunity to refine, clarify, and strengthen the strategy.

This is easier said than done! So, to make it actionable, we've broken it down into six people-focused steps:

Step	Definition
1. Enroll People	Bring people into the possibility of change.
2. Feel the Vision	Clarify direction and build commitment.
3. Increase Capability	Develop new awareness, skills, systems required to drive change.
4. Experiment with Possibility	Test new methods, apply and innovate.
5. Celebrate Progress	Clarify what's happened and bring that to the surface.
6. Re-Imagine the Future	Update the future vision based on progress to date.

So finally we can complete the model by adding these six steps, as shown on the following page.

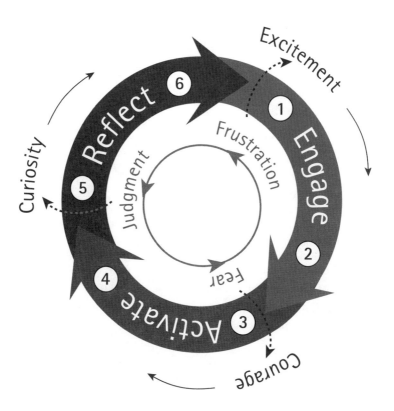

We call this the Change MAP – MAP for Management Process. It's a framework we use to design and manage change – whether we're talking about an hour-long process of changing awareness or a three-year large-scale transformation.

✔ The goal is to "spin the wheel" and get the virtuous spiral growing stronger and faster – without skipping any phase.

In practice, we'll "spin the wheel" many times in any project as well as structure the whole with the MAP. For example, in one iteration of the cycle designing a learning project, we might have:

> **Engage**: Planning meeting (structured based on the three phases).

> **Activate**: Two-day workshop followed by coaching: Each day of the workshop (and within that, each module), and each coaching session, is built around the three phases.

> **Reflect**: Follow the three phases in a 2-hour wrap-up session and prepare for next steps.

So the whole project is planned using the MAP, and each component also uses the MAP… and subcomponents can also follow the same MAP. This fractal-like approach creates an iterative process that builds positive momentum and increases clarity.

Later in the chapter we'll provide three brief case studies showing the application of the Change MAP.

How-To

Most of our clients come from highly "IQ-driven" backgrounds – finance, engineering, research, etc. While they might "get" that leadership is largely about people, their default thinking is more mechanistic. So we've broken the Change MAP into a logical structure that will make implementation more systematic.

To make the model more easily actionable, within each step there are two milestones.

Phase	Steps	Milestones
Engage	1. Enroll people	Understand the Drivers
		Create Hope
	2. Feel the Vision	Draft the Map
		Invite to Change
Activate	3. Increase Capability	Expand Competencies
		Prepare to Launch
	4. Experiment with Possibility	Jump In
		Strengthen Support
Reflect	5. Celebrate Progress	Discover Results
		Share Lessons Learned
	6. Re-Imagine the Future	Integrate Achievements
		Look Forward

Finally, within each milestone there are a variety of actions that can be taken to reach the milestone. In Part Two, we present the model in detail, including four actions for each milestone in an "operation manual" for each phase.

This logical chart is helpful, but:

 Remember the Change MAP is a cycle.

Levels of Awareness

There's one more critical dimension to the Change MAP, which is an explicit recognition that as social beings we exist within relationships and in a larger systemic context. Likewise, our organizations are made up of relationships, made up of individuals. This dynamic is represented by three expanding rings:

At the base, the first ring is the individual – you, or any individual person. The second ring is the relational, a group of people who have some interaction and bond. The third is the organization or systemic. The arrow through the middle represents an alignment toward a purpose.

✔ Ideally all three rings are working together synergistically to achieve something worthwhile; that accomplishment will not fully succeed without all three levels.

It's also important to note that the three levels inherently and automatically affect one another. In the next chapter explaining the science and theory behind the model, we'll talk about "emotional contagion," the automatic transmission of emotion from one person to another, which is one of the ways the levels interact. In any case, changes at any one level will affect the other two.

Finally, we'd like to ask you to consider yourself in these three rings. Which gets your attention? Most people are most comfortable in one level, and perhaps "conversant" within another, but very few can comfortably and smoothly move between all three.

Many executives are great at the "organizational" ring – they look at spreadsheets and org charts like a breathing entity that they deeply understand, and they see a clear path to change. Then, when you ask, "How would that affect you, individually?", it's like you're speaking a foreign language.

Others, such as strong HR managers, seem most comfortable in the "relational" ring – they immediately see the dynamics in a team; they can put their finger on what's driving that group's behavior. But they may have trouble scaling that into a strategic, organizational perspective.

And finally, some people, counselors are a good example, are most effective looking at individuals-as-individuals. Each is unique, mysterious, and enthralling. However, when you ask these people to talk to a whole group, they are way outside their comfort zone.

✔ As a truly effective EQ change leader, you will need to be able to see and manage all three levels.

Case Stories

To help make the Change MAP more clear, we'd like to share three examples of how the model has worked in three different kinds of interventions: organizational, team and individual.

Organizational Case:

Optimizing Manufacturing Reengineering with a Change MAnagement Process (Change MAP)

This case is about a leading global chemical company dedicated to producing high-value benefits for its customers' products. In 2008, the company's continued operations generated sales of US$5.2 billion and invested more than US$200 million in R&D.

Background:

In 2006 a major reorganization program, called Operational Agenda, was launched to improve company profitability. The program included several initiatives such as implementation of SAP, Lean Manufacturing, a new geographical footprint and a new concept and structure for innovation, marketing and sales.

The manufacturing plant near Bologna, Italy, which produces a variety highly specialized products in a highly competitive global market, was part of the Operational Agenda initiative. Senior plant leadership recognized the breadth and the complexity of the change and the need to fully engage people in the process. They decided to fuse the implementation of the Agenda with a change management initiative. The Change MAP was designed to support the managers to understand the reaction of personnel during these major changes, to engage the middle managers by gaining their commitment, and to enlarge the base of the "change agents."

Implementation:

Before launching this iteration of the cycle, we went through the three phases several times – first with the site leader and then the leader plus his senior team. From those Change MAP processes, we planned this implementation:

1. Engage

Senior and middle managers participated in an outdoor strategic workshop resulting in all managers recognizing and appropriately expressing their feelings, building a common vision and becoming committed as change agents.

During the preparation of the meeting, we worked extensively with the Site Manager to understand the people's possible reactions and how to create a compelling and motivating call for change.

The workshop started with a recap of the Operational Agenda and an exercise to support people to openly discuss their feelings about change. Fear, anger, and, for some, enthusiasm were the most used words. The managers talked about the challenge of the change and about the opportunities it provided. The purpose of the change was explained and clarified and the Site Leader shared the draft of the Change MAP asking people to work together to refine it. The last part of the workshop was dedicated to the call for action: are you ready to facilitate change? If yes, let's take the ownership of the project!

Their assignment as change agents provided a focus to mentor employees to "buy in" to the company and the transformation.

2. Activate

A combination of a capability development program and "on the job consulting" supported managers to address the issues raised in the ongoing change efforts:

Training sessions were delivered so managers could focus on individual employees' responses to change. We started with the emotional side of change and how the brain is functioning in order to support people in understanding their own reactions, and to figure out potential reactions of their employees. After that we created a set of tools for change agents: a practical guide for the leadership of change. This safe environment provided a venue to share individual experiences about change and create a learning community, a powerful vehicle to maintain a strong, supportive team spirit.

During every management meeting the consultants focused attention on the people side of change. This process led to a better understanding of critical issues and perceptions of leadership. The managers were encouraged to hold coaching and consultancy discussions on specific issues with key employees.

The training and coaching sessions, and planning meetings, were structured using the Engage, Activate, Reflect phases, so in this project there were many iterations of the cycle.

3. Reflect

The company's commitment to change was monitored with a continuous attention to results and people's motivation, periodically adjusting and fine-tuning when necessary. At the end of this period, we assessed the people-side with the Organizational Vital Signs assessment (OVS), a tool designed to understand the emotional dynamics of a change and important outcomes: Retention, Productivity and Customer Service.

The Site Leader held a review session where the overall results of the process were presented to celebrate, share the lessons learned and define the next steps. The leadership team then had a new "Engage" meeting to prepare the next iteration of the cycle, which is ongoing.

Effectiveness:

Commitment to the Change MAP assisted the company to achieve important business goals—for example, over two years, productivity increased by 18% with a 15% cost reduction in headcount while simultaneously reducing complaints by 73%.

Plant leaders attribute the efficacy of the program to combining the potential of the "rational" tools from SAP, Lean Manufacturing, and business re-engineering fused with the people insights and tools of the Change MAP. It's exceptional to see such strong, positive engagement at the end of a business turnaround; this is the evidence that it is possible to successfully change an organization.

The site manager's summary: "One plus one makes three: that's the power of the Change MAP in a big organizational change!"

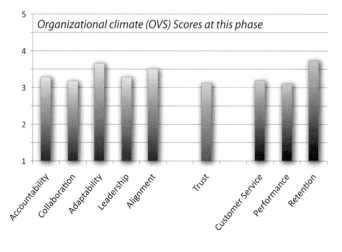

Organizational climate (OVS) Scores at this phase

Team Case

Managerial Team Development with Change MAnagement Program (Change MAP)

In this case we used the MAP with a management team to increase effectiveness. The client's business is the development, manufacture, and sales of health care products for use in clinical and home settings with 41,000 employees located in 59 countries worldwide.

Background:

In 2009 we were asked to create a development program for the management team. The situation was critical; the level of conflict inside the team was growing day by day. The CEO was really worried about the future of the company and he was unsure how to manage this complicated situation.

We proposed to use the Change MAP in the design of the program.

Implementation:

As in the previous example, this implementation follows after several cycles of the MAP with the CEO and various team members. As the result of these initial cycles, together we planned this next iteration.

1. Engage

The CEO invited the management team to join us for a workshop about the people-side of business. In the presentation, the CEO pointed out his perceptions about the state of the team and asked us to support the team in finding a way to improve collaboration. We discussed change, best practices, and we shared some opportunities to create a new climate. We asked them to follow up by taking a survey to have a clear snapshot of the situation.

Every team member received a link for the Team Vital Signs (TVS), a tool to assess the engagement of the members around collaboration, execution, innovation, trust and so on. The survey results were presented in a two-hour debriefing meeting to the overall team. As you can imagine, the results were not positive. We asked the team members how they felt about the data, and almost all expressed that they were not satisfied with the status quo. So we presented them a program to improve collaboration. The CEO gave them the responsibility to decide if they wanted to go ahead with the program or not. It was up to them. There was an opportunity to work on the team climate but they were free to choose. The answer was yes.

2. Activate

A blended learning program was delivered:

We started with a two-day class about personal change and the dynamics of emotions. Preparation for the workshop included two assessments, the SEI (an EQ Leadership competency measure) and a 360 assessing the effects of current EQ performance.

Next came three one-to-one coaching meetings to discuss the results of questionnaires and to define an individual development plan.

After approximately two months of focus at the individual level, we turned to explore the team dynamics in a two-day outdoor training. We experienced a lot of stressful and exciting challenges to reflect on the team reactions. In the last half-day we defined a goal to reach in the next month, as a team.

In the final month the team worked on the goal with the support of personal coaches; meanwhile we supported the CEO in facilitating the team dynamics to reinforce the key components of the trainings.

3. Reflect

A month after the project's conclusion, we had a follow up review of what happened. We asked people to express their feelings about the work they did together and to give one another feedback. In the last part of the meeting, they decided how to continue working on the team effectiveness for the next year, paving the way for the next cycle through the MAP.

Effectiveness:

The team achieved strong results. They were able to overcome almost all the personal struggles and concentrate on the business issues. This focus permitted them to reach a gold level in the Worldwide Manufactory Excellence Program, and site productivity was better then ever.

The CEO's comment was, "I have had proof of the impact of people in the business!"

Individual Case

Leader Development with Change MAnagement Program (Change MAP)

We worked with the CEO of a regional bank to increase effectiveness. The company serves over 60,000 customers across 12 branches.

Background:

Initially we me with the CEO and followed the stages of the MAP to identify key needs. She recognized that while her brand proposition was all about relationship, the senior executive team was not modeling an ideal relationship. We then defined a plan and cemented her commitment to create change.

Implementation:

After several iterations of the MAP with the CEO and COO preparing the way, we followed the three phases to turn a corner:

1. Engage

In a session with the CEO's team, we asked them to envision their ideal situation as a team and the critical gaps between the current reality and that vision. In a coaching session with the CEO the same day, we asked her to identify a specific goal for herself and her team of 10 people, not the organization as a whole.

2. Activate

Together we planned to administer the SEI 360 (a tool to collect feedback on performance with emotional intelligence) to gather input from the team. We used the CEO's 360 as a way of showing the team members the process because we wanted each of them to do the same in the next cycle of change. So the CEO carefully communicated her goals in doing the 360, which was the first step in setting up her change.

The results of the 360 were positive overall, but the CEO saw a particular gap in several areas. Here is the feedback on "Apply Consequential Thinking," the competence for carefully evaluating the tactical and emotional impact of decisions before acting:

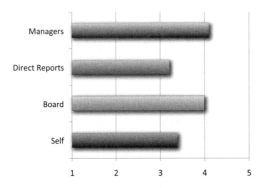

Overall, others perceived a positive performance in the emotional domain; her scores are well above the performance target for this competence. However, in this graph and many others, her Direct Reports were providing much lower scores than others in the organization.

After a 1:1 coaching session to review the feedback and plan, we had another meeting with the team and discussed: What does leadership look like? This meeting was also structured around the MAP, beginning with an Engage discussion on trust and the brand, and ending with a Reflection on each person's commitment to growth. The CEO shared her perception of the 360 feedback saying that she decided it was time to "step up" as a leader of the team.

We had additional coaching and meetings around this goal. The CEO is a very warm, genuine, people-oriented leader, and part of the challenge was to be a bit tougher on her team.

3. Reflect

Before moving on to the next phase of the MAP, conducting 360s with the rest of the team, we met to review the results in process. The CEO had tracked "micrometrics" to see how often she was following through on specific commitments, and saw strong progress. She was also able to confront some specific people where there was no longer an ideal fit, and made some changes in the team.

Effectiveness:

In discussions with team members (in the next cycle of the MAP), many noticed a real change in the CEO's interactions with them and the team. The CEOs summary: "I have already seen a huge shift on my team. We'll continue to go through the change process." Like many banks around the globe, they faced a seriously challenging period in 2009. The CEO wrote us near the end of the year: "I wanted to share with you that the work we did last year has certainly helped us get through these tough times."

Recap

The Change MAP distills change theory into a practical action-learning process that helps leaders guide and sustain change. One key differentiator is designing change through a "Ready, Fire, Aim" model focused on continuous improvement.

Another essential is recognizing and providing a framework for skillfully managing the emotions that cause people to either resist or embrace change. The process helps managers develop a commitment to shared vision of a better organization, implement new initiatives while managing resistance, and then build clarity and alignment in a continuous improvement process.

The "secret" to this model is treating emotion as a valuable part of change. Some emotions can give us insight and push us for change. Other emotions can fuel change and sustain the change process.

The final differentiator is putting people at the center of the change process, following the deployment of the six steps to reach the goals. The effective way to change an organization is to understand how people change. Thus the work of the change leader isn't to push past feelings that are "in the way," but rather to mine the value and power of emotions in order to build forward momentum in three phases:

> "Engage" is about getting ready – gathering ideas, resources, strategies, and emotional buy-in.

> "Activate" is about baby-step implementation - increasing capacity by adding new awareness and skills.

> "Reflect" is about refining – re-assessing and improving the plans.

Change leaders must understand how this process occurs on multiple levels: Within themselves, together in teams, and across an organization. Following the Change MAP and attending to these three levels will shift the organization forward – incrementally and continuously.

There are many competencies required for successful change. Strategic thinking, analysis, relationship-building, and project management are required. In addition, there is a fundamentally human component of change operating at an emotional level.

Emotional intelligence provides powerful insights and tools for engaging people in accomplishing critical goals. Emotional intelligence (or "EQ") is the capacity to effectively use emotions, and it's a key factor differentiating successful leaders.

The only difference

between a rut and a grave

is their dimensions.

– Ellen Glasgow

Chapter 3:
Current Science

There is so much to learn about how people work. In the last decade we've seen an explosion of neuroscience that's transforming our understanding of human behavior and motivation. Meanwhile, many "experts" cling to old paradigms and models, and surely we do that to some extent as well. So it may not be possible to know "the truth" about how people work, but it's certainly possible to be a student of people – to approach the puzzle of change as a learner. In the context of change, there are several critical areas for understanding:

1. Learning – basic insights into the way the human brain processes information and stimuli

2. Interacting – how emotions affect people and people affect emotions

3. Achieving – the result of successful emotional interaction is trust, the currency of emotional effectiveness

Learning

The real challenges of change are rooted in neurobiology – the human brain literally wires itself to respond a particular way. The patterns of thought, feeling, and action quickly form, based on experience, and slowly change – it's our brain's way of making life easy. To overcome the brain's wiring, sometimes a company needs a fairly radical culture change.

Since the neurological patterns form based on experience, corporate culture tends to be self-reinforcing – people come to see a particular way of doing business as normal, and normal feels right. But business-normal is often dysfunctional.

A terrific example is the W.L. Gore Company founded in 1958 by Bill and Vieve Gore – makers of the waterproof fabric GORE-TEX, widely used in outdoor gear,. Bill realized, while working at Dupont, that there were only two places where people really collaborated: an informal taskforce and a carpool. All the other situations were affected by hierarchy and roles. He tried to create a new company with a new culture: no hierarchy, only teamwork. When a new Associate (not "employee") comes into the company, they're told, "We have no bosses here." At first the new people think that that's just corporate talk and euphemism, and for a time they keep asking, "No, really – who's my boss?" Eventually they begin to "unlearn" the old patterns and adapt to the Gore culture.[18]

Now almost 50 years old with over $1.8B in sales, 45 plants, and nine years near the top of Fortune's 100 Best Places to Work, the experiment seems to be a success. In terms of change, what's interesting about the Gore case is an illustration of the power of patterns. The conceptual framework starts at a neurological level with brain cells connecting to form interlocking systems. Those new Gore employees have the system of "boss" and "hierarchy" strongly connected with the notion of "work." The patterns become a kind of frame though which they see the world, and their brains literally restructure so that frame makes sense. Then, when they come into W.L. Gore, they have to rewire that frame; they're told "this is different," but only through prolonged experience does that way of seeing change.

This type of learning, reconnecting neural systems, is what neuroscientists call "neuroplasticity" – the brain is changeable, and first-hand experience over a period of time is a powerful way to rewire the synapses. Neural connections develop and change in response to environmental stimulus.[19] Patterns form unconsciously and automatically, but they also can be shaped intentionally.

 The first step to changing patterns is recognizing them, a conscious appraisal of thoughts, feelings, and reactions. This requires self-reflection – or "zooming back" to see a larger picture.

Inside the Brain

The brain is made up of billions of interconnected networks, each carrying a dynamic mix of concepts associated with feelings. The connections are "plastic;" the brain is constantly reforming based on the way it's used. In 1/10,000,000th of a second a neuron can change its connection. Neurons that "fire together, wire together" – so when we associate particular concepts or feelings with one another, we reinforce a connection.

These connections are formed through hundreds or millions of "micro-bridges" between one network and another; the more bridges, the stronger the association. Change often involves rewiring these bridges, and that's one reason it takes time – spread over time.

Because of neuroplasticity, the brain is constantly changing – a great deal in childhood, but it doesn't end there. All our lives the brain changes as we learn and adapt to new challenges. A macro example is that someone can have a brain injury to their language centers, even an adult whose language center is fully developed, and in many cases he can learn to speak again. A micro example is that someone who doesn't know how to use his new iPhone can quickly learn. To make these new bridges, to use the plasticity, we need focus and attention – readiness, the right environment, and then stimulus. Intelligence is due to the development of neural connections responding to the environment, and differences in intelligence are due to difference in this adaptation process.[20]

Once neuroscientists thought that you were born with a fixed number of neurons (brain cells), but now we know they are produced throughout our lives. We don't know exactly how to speed up this production, but physical and mental activity seems to be key (along with healthy diet). Your body's muscles atrophy without use and strengthen with activity, your brain responds in similar ways.[21]

Six principles of neuroscience and change:

1. Our brains love patterns. They create efficiency. Changing patterns requires "stepping back" from the day-to-day. Change can occur only when you are paying attention, so you need to engage people's brains so they focus on the change.

2. Initial change is only temporary. Repetition is a key to strengthen connections between neurons. It needs to be incremental and reinforced. Stress increases the likelihood of returning to the old way.

3. The brain needs exercise to flourish. Both mental exercise (thinking, feeling), and physical exercise (to increase oxygen). Sleep and diet also have a dramatic impact on brain function.

4. Neuroplasticity is a two-way street. We can learn new habits that are positive and productive, we can also learn habits that are negative and destructive. The brain is accommodating and it will become efficient and effective with either set of habits.

5. Emotion drives learning, providing a regulatory function, a "reality check," and a way of saying "pay attention." What we care about, we focus on – what we focus on, we remember.

6. Emotion is motivating. When we feel a sense of commitment, we focus and engage more deeply.

The Science of Learning

There are many researchers looking to understand how we learn, and how, specifically, the brain processes new information. Marcus E. Raichle, for example, studied people learning new words then repeating the words later. Using fMRI and PET scans, he was able to see the actual brain centers involved in new learning versus those involved in using something already learned. In the past, theorists believed that we practice something until it becomes deeply entrenched, but Raichle's work shows that's not quite right. When we learn something new, certain brain areas are heavily involved (including the "executive" areas of the prefrontal cortex that manage evaluative processes), but then the learning is passed into other areas; we practice with one part of our brain and plant the new data into another portion of the brain that will be active during unconscious, everyday activity. When we focus our attention on learning something new, it appears that we actually suppress activity in those "everyday" regions. This suppression can begin before we actually encounter the new data as we anticipate the new input.[22]

This means that we can prepare for learning and, essentially, quiet the mind to focus on what's new. The implication is not staggering: we need focused, calm attention for learning. But given that most organizations attempt to "fix the car while it's driving 60 miles an hour," we have new insight into why organizational learning so frequently fails.

We usually think of new ideas and current situations filtering through the brain into memory like a video camera. But really it's a two-way process: The brain expects a new situation to be like what we've experienced in the past, so signals come from our memories into the parts of the brain where we experience sensory input – preparing us to re-experience those remembered senses.[23] The result is that the past becomes part of our filter in the present, and we mix and blend imagination, memory, and current experience. This means we have to put in extra effort to really see what's new and different – one reason quantitative feedback is so valuable in change.

Regina Pally, a researcher at UCLA, studies the way the brain responds to improve therapeutic treatment. One of her findings is of particular importance in terms of change. Because our brains love to make and follow patterns to increase efficiency, we have a variety of systems that help us predict what is going to happen next. The problem is that these tend to reinforce the past rather then prepare us for something new.

In Pally's words, "In a sense, we learn from the past what to predict for the future and then live the future we expect."[24] When we re-create the past experience in our brains, Pally explains, we experience that as real. For most areas of the brain, whatever we experience **is** reality – it's like in the movie, *The Matrix*: What we imagine is the reality we experience. It takes intensive effort of testing and re-evaluating to distinguish between our map of reality and others' maps of reality. Each of our maps, moreover, is largely driven by our past experience being continuously replayed and reinforced. That makes it challenging to adapt to new situations; again, we have to step back from the everyday process and deliberately move into a new state where we can reflect.

So how do we change that map? Can we simply "unlearn" it? Apparently not: Instead, we create new learning on top of the old map, essentially annotating the old map with corrections, a process that requires conscious, focused thought.[25] "That street is closed, go this way instead." 'Unlearning' actually causes the growth of new brain connections in the prefrontal cortex, which serve to inhibit the original conditioned learning.[26]
One problem with this system is that the old map is still there, and generally the old map is very familiar! So when we're

stressed or rushed, we might forget to "read the corrections" and follow the old map – even though we "know" it's incorrect.

Paradoxically, perhaps, one function of emotion is to help us test our maps against others' and "stay in reality." Emotions provide a regulatory function helping us measure our choices against our own reactions and the reactions of others. When people disconnect from their emotions, their decision-making becomes impaired. For example, in a study of people suffering from the eating disorder, Anorexia Nervosa, they are less aware of their feelings (in fact, are more likely to exhibit signs of clinical emotional suppression called alexithymia), and they are less able to recognize others' emotions.[27]

The study also found that treatment was more effective when patients were better able to soothe their own emotions; in other words, if the patients felt anxious they ignored their feelings, but when they were able to relax themselves they could benefit from the valuable information and energy provided by their feelings. The implication for change is that if we attend to our emotions when they're relatively new and subtle, we'll get more value than if we wait for the raging storm.

This requires close attention. Emotional arousal – feeling something – is actually the brain's way of signaling: Something is happening! The hippocampus, the part of the brain responsible for attention control, is particularly sensitive to emotional changes. And when our emotion fades, so does attention. There are particular parts of the brain that create attention, and simply put, when we get bored we stop paying attention.[28] The implication, though, is important for us as change leaders:

 By creating and maintaining emotional engagement, we increase the capacity to pay attention.

The risk is to remain in our comfort zone. Learning new tasks and moving into challenge is key to activating and using our brains fully. But too much challenge creates distress, which shuts down learning. Practice is key – repetition reinforces a new way of using the brain making it more and more automatic.

Interacting

Emotions are contagious. Because we are pack animals, we've adapted to be highly sensitive to opportunities and threats that affect the group. Emotions form a nearly instant transmission system carrying survival data throughout the pack. One person's feelings WILL affect others, and people are especially prone to pick up on feelings from those they like/admire and from those in power. Change often involves changing the culture and climate – the rules and the feelings – that drive group behavior, so it's essential to recognize and monitor the effect of emotional contagion. In turn, these feeling signals interact, changing how we feel and also how we perceive situations involving others.

One of the biggest challenges in change is managing our interpretations and assumptions about others. Behavior, by itself, is fairly neutral – someone walks out of the room, no big deal. But if we decide, "he walked out of the room because he's ignoring me," we feel disrespected, even betrayed, and now the stakes go up; emotionally, the gun is loaded. The challenge: We don't KNOW what someone else is feeling, but we react as if we did. As Regina Pally describes it:

 "In social interaction, we react not to another's behavior, but to their intention, which we predict."[29]

We do this prediction unconsciously and automatically. We have a type of brain cell, called a "mirror neuron," that is particularly involved in interaction with others. One function of mirror neurons is to monitor others' behavior. Mirror neurons are linked to our motor (behavioral) centers, but also to our emotional centers. They track what others are doing and how we feel about that. An intriguing study by mirror-neuron pioneer Marco Iacoboni used fMRI to track responses to when participants watched a video of someone grasping a coffee cup with different intentions (sometimes to drink, sometimes to clean it).

Iacoboni and team were able to see how the brain was predicting and ascribing intention. The study found that, in essence, we predict someone's intention based on how *we* might feel doing what they're doing.[30] We map, in our brains, what might be happening in their brains, and then we say, "what would I do next, and why would I do that?" Then we assume that's what *they* would do next and why. This can create a kind of blindness; we "know" that others feel the same as we do. The implication is that, especially in times of complexity (like change), we need to be careful to actually ask about others' intentions.

Given the importance of these two areas – mirror neurons and emotional contagion – we'll explore them in more depth.

Mirror Neurons

Studies show that individuals receive, encode, and interpret information pertaining to the knowledge and perspectives of others. As players within a social context, we as humans attend to the experiences of those around us and use our observations to make predictions of others' behaviors and reactions to various environments and events.

Several theories have historically sought to explain the unique ability of humans to "step inside the shoes" of others. Over the years, developmental psychologists have shown that children as young as three are able to accurately assess the mental states and perspectives of other people.[31] That is, not only do children have an understanding that the knowledge of others may differ from their own, but also they are able to incorporate their knowledge of others' perspectives to make estimates of others' mental and emotional states.

More recently, advancements in neural imaging technology have allowed researchers to investigate humans' sensitivity to others from an alternative, neurobiological, perspective. Research performed originally with primates has suggested that nerve cells within the brain may play a key role in humans' aptitude in sharing experiences and emotions.

The Mirror Neuron System

Mirror neurons were first discovered in the 1990s by researchers at the university in Parma, Italy. Originally using macaque monkeys as their participants, scientists accidentally discovered that when the monkeys observed specific physical actions (e.g. grasping, chewing, and biting) being performed by a peer, specific nerve cells within the brain would become active in the same way as if they themselves were performing the action.[32] These nerve cells, called mirror neurons, are thought to represent the biological link between individuals during communication.[33]

Although the field of mirror neuron research is in its infancy, several key scientists have suggested that there may be a biological basis for the spread of emotion between individuals.[34] Gallese argues that another's emotion is directly experienced by an observer by means of similarities in neural activity; that is, people can directly understand and experience the emotional states of others because their brain cells will react in analogous ways.

 We are wired to experience others' emotions.

Furthermore, and as should be expected, activations in mirror areas of the brain are shown to be related to ability in perspective taking.[35] In a recent study conducted in the Netherlands, 16 subjects were exposed to recorded sounds associated with two manual actions. In the following sitting, participants were asked to perform actions similar to the ones whose sounds they had heard during the previous sitting. fMRI data from the experiment showed not only that specific areas of the left hemisphere are activated by both the sound and experience of specific actions, but that this system was activated more so for participants who scored higher on an empathy scale. In other words, there is a direct link between the mirror activity, the motor activity, and the emotional activity.

These findings beg the question: Is one's ability to respond to others' emotional cues biologically fixed, or can it improve over time? Luckily, research suggests that we are not restricted by the abilities of our mirror neuron systems, but that repeated and persistent stimulation may result in improved ability to detect and experience others' emotions.[36]

The implication of the mirror system is critical for all leaders, but especially change leaders:

✔ Not only are people watching, but their brains are literally mapping your reactions.

Just by walking in the room, you affect people's brains – they are, we all are, wired to connect. This system fuels the transfer of emotions between people, what scientists call "emotional contagion."

Emotional Contagion

In daily interactions with people at home, work, and in the community, people unconsciously send messages about how they are feeling while simultaneously receiving the emotional messages being sent by others. Recent research has verified that these emotional cues affect each person's own moods, and in turn, these feelings affect how they perform.

Systems of Mood Contagion

Studies of mood and human behavior have shown that feelings spread from one person to another through a number of mechanisms. For example, factors of non-verbal communication including facial expressions, posture, and specific behavioral patterns have all been linked to the transmission of emotional information between individuals.[37] In addition, recent studies have shown that mood can spread through aspects of verbal communication such as voice inflection.[38]

In a recent study by Neumann and Strack, participants were

asked to listen to an emotionally impartial speech read by an actor using happy, sad, or neutral voice inflection. When later asked to rate their emotions, participants reported having emotions consistent with those of the speaker. Furthermore, when asked to rate their attitude toward the speaker, participants consistently liked the speaker with the sad voice least $F(2,26) = 11.08, p < .001$ (see Figure 1).[38]

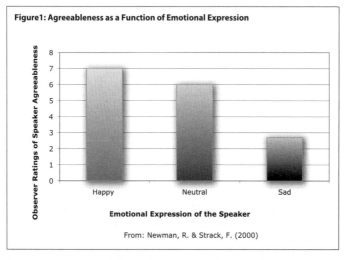

Figure1: Agreeableness as a Function of Emotional Expression

From: Newman, R. & Strack, F. (2000)

Are humans born with this innate sensitivity to the emotions of others? Some scientists would argue yes. Newborn infants have been shown to physically imitate the facial expressions of their caregivers. While some have interpreted this as an indication of instinctual emotional sensitivity,[39] it appear that our sensitivity to the feelings of others develops over time and is adapted and perfected with experience.[40] This means we can learn to become more effective at reading this important "universal human language" of emotional interplay.

Mood Contagion Within Groups
· ·

With clear applications within business, social, and personal settings, mood contagion has become an important class of group dynamics research. In 2002, Sigal Barsade of Yale University examined the effect of emotional contagion within the workplace team context. In her experiment, a trained actor was secretly included in each group and directed to participate in the groups' activities while enacting varying levels of pleasantness and energy. The groups were working to assign pay a pay bonus; they had a fixed amount of money they could spend and had to allocate it based on a set of performance criteria. After the activities were completed, participants were asked to complete self-assessments of their mood. The actor's mood affected the group mood – and the group performance. Results of the study clearly suggested that the effect of one group member's emotions had an unconscious effect on the mood of the other group members. This held true both for "positive" and "negative" moods.[41]

There are different opinions of the effect of positional power / authority on mood contagion. It may be that those with authority and those who are either liked or respected have a greater effect. What is clear is that leaders affect the group mood:

> "In a study of the influence of the contagion of mood of a group leader on group members, the positive mood of the leader positively influenced group members at both the individual and collective level with the opposite for leader negative mood. The leader's positive mood also had a subsequent influence on group coordination and effort." - Sy, Côté, & Saavedra, 2005[42]

The Effect of Mood
. . . .

Given that mood is contagious, one important consideration is the effect of mood on performance. Some authors focus on the idea that "positive" moods have a positive effect on performance, but, in reality, sometimes a "negative" mood is appropriate.

In the Barsade study discussed above, a negative group member seemed to disrupt the groups and reduce efficacy, while having a positive confederate was associated with increased cooperation, fewer group conflicts, and heightened task performance. Likewise, in a similar study, Alice Isen assessed radiologists, finding positive mood enhanced their accuracy. Positive mood has a far-reaching effect on work performance, supervision, decision-making, and even on team members voluntarily acting for the good of the organization.[43]

On the other hand, in some situations a "bad mood" is more effective. For example, Elsbach and Barr found that people in negative moods use a more structured approach to decision-making. Their summary of mood effects is shown below in Table 1.[44]

 Mood changes performance – the right mood enhances it, the wrong mood undermines it.

Table 1: Findings on the Effects of Positive and Negative Moods on Decision Making[44]

Positive Mood:

Potential Benefits	Potential Costs
• Cues positive materials in memory (Isen et al. 1978) • Promotes creative problem solving (Isen et al. 1987) • Promotes more flexible categorization of items (Isen & Daubman, 1984) • Promotes efficiency in decision-making (isen & Means, 1983) • Promotes thoroughness in interesting tasks (Isen et al, 1991)	• Promotes risk aversion, more negative subjective utility for losses (Isen et al. 1988) • Promotes use of heuristics and quick decision-making (Isen & Means, 1983) • Difficulty discerning weak and strong arguments (Smith & Shaffer, 1991(• Persuaded by peripheral cues (e.g., "expert" label) (Mackie & Worth, 1991) • Less likely to use a structured decision protocol completely and correctly (Elsbach & Barr, 1999)

Negative Mood

Potential Benefits	Potential Costs
• Not affected by distractions and engage in more message elaboration (Bless et al, 1990)	• Reliance on well-known decision rules (Mano, 1992)
• Less likely to rely on peripheral cues (Worth & Mackle, 1987)	• Increased pessimism (Wright & Bower, 1992)
• Motivated to engage in effortful analysis to change situation & mood (Bless et al., 1990)	• Increased negative judgments of others (Fiske & Taylor, 1984)
• More likely to use a structured decision protocol completely and correctly (Elsbach & Barr, 1999)	• Risk-taking when potential benefits/losses are large (Dunegan et al., 1992)

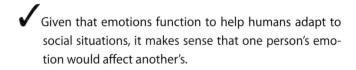 Given that emotions function to help humans adapt to social situations, it makes sense that one person's emotion would affect another's.

Just as pack animals would benefit from rapidly passing messages about risk and reward, emotional contagion seems to be adaptive for humans to function in groups. This system can enable a rapid communication of opportunity and risk, mediate a group interaction, and help humans attend to social rules and norms such as maintaining harmonious interaction with a powerful ally.

The evidence that an individual's feelings affects others – and that these feelings in turn affect performance – illustrates the importance of being aware of and managing emotions. This is especially important for leaders, educators, salespeople, parents, politicians, athletes – really any person concerned with their influence on others.

One challenge is that the emotional exchange will occur even without conscious attention. In other words, whether they know it or not, people are affecting one another. If emotional intelligence allows people to monitor and manage this exchange, developing emotional intelligence will improve people's ability to successfully interact with others.

Achieving

If we are effective in using our emotional interaction in organizational life, one result will be increased trust.

Each and every day, in millions of human interactions, trust plays an essential role in our lives. Our world revolves around trust: we trust that street lights will be red for cross traffic when it is green for us; we trust that we will receive our paychecks at the end of a month's labor; we trust that our dentist is being truthful when he says he must drill out a cavity; we trust that our currency has value. When we talk about change, trust is even more important: We need to experience a high degree of trust when we change jobs, when we change houses, when we change habits. Trust is the hope behind change.

Trust is a risk, as Hong & Bohnet write: "Trust is the willingness to make the self vulnerable to others."[45] While most of us know what it is and have experienced the "feel" of trust or distrust, it's challenging to measure. Even more difficult is to explain our reasons for experiencing trust. Recent studies have attempted to uncover the cognitive, behavioral, and physiological variables contributing to the presence or absence of trust.

What Trust Enables and How to Create It

There is an element of trust that is cultural. Researcher Paul Zak found varying trust levels in different nations. The same, presumably, would then be true in different organizational cultures. The norms and expectations, the background knowledge and people's feelings about those norms, will affect how and when trust is given. Moreover, the more ethno-linguistic homogeneity that exists in a country, the more trust is apparent.[46] The implication is that in an increasingly globalized and diverse business world, trust will be even more challenging to establish.

What's happens at an individual level?

If an individual gives resources to another without a corresponding commitment or obligation on the part of the other person, trust is inherently implied. However, understanding the subtle mechanisms and processes driving trust is a whole different story.

Ralph Adolphs discovered that the amygdala (which drives emotional reactions to threat) is more activated when people see faces that they rated as untrustworthy. So the perception of trust has an impact on our emotional brains, and our emotions affect the perception of trust. For example, expressions of anger and sadness are negatively correlated with trustworthiness; happiness is positively correlated.[47] This is an important finding for a leader: do you want to be trusted? Pay attention to your emotion. We will discuss this further in the third section of the book.

Recent research by Kosfeld, et. al., 2005, provides more evidence that trust has some chemical/biological origins. This study found that subjects who were given the neuropeptide oxytocin were significantly more trusting than control subjects.[48] Oxytocin is commonly known as a mammalian hormone, found in high levels in birthing and breastfeeding females; it creates a desire for social cohesion. Biologically speaking, this makes sense, as a pregnant or lactating female must place trust in others, most specifically her partner, to protect and provide for her and her infant. Perhaps oxytocin could be called the trust hormone!

Several studies have also shown that trust begets trust.[49] One individual displays trust by offering resources to a trustee, the trustee may feel encouraged to give back, thereby demonstrating trust. As reported in an important study by Zak, Kurzban and Matzner, those who received a signal of intentional trust from others had almost twice the level of oxytocin as the control group – so **receiving trust generates some of the same biological response as giving trust**.[50]

Another interesting finding is that the level of oxytocin is not related to demographics, social behaviors and psychological profiles. So we can say there is a cultural trust due to history and experience but there is no difference at the individual level from the biological point of view. This means we can throw out many of our stereotypes based on race or nationality, and instead assess trust based on individual relationships. The most highly correlated variable associated with generalized trust is self-reported happiness.[51] So if we want trusting relationships, we can use happiness as a benchmark.

Of critical importance in change is the relationship between fear and trust. In a subsequent study, Baumgarner et. al. found that oxytocin causes selective deactivation in fear circuitry.[52] So, trust is an antidote to fear. Also, individuals who dislike risk show less trusting behavior,[53] so trust is key to risk-taking. From these studies we can deduce that trust may be established when an individual's ability to recognize or perceive fear is reduced, and their desire and feeling of social connectedness is increased. Hence trust mitigates the effects of fear and increases willingness to join the group – even when that involves risk.

From the perspective of a change leader, neurobiology is giving us important clues about the link between affect (emotion) and behavior. If we want people to change, certain emotional ingredients will be required.

Recap

Critical components of change include learning, group dynamics, and trust. Using current neuroscience as a foundation, change leaders will be more effective working on the people-side of the equation.

Remember:

- Change begins in the brain. The brain is "plastic" – it changes itself. Intentional change, or learning, requires focused attention, repetition, reinforcement and just enough challenge.

- Emotion drives attention and shapes how the individual and groups respond. Emotion is contagious, literally mapping between one person and another as a "biological instant messaging" system.

- Trust is reciprocal, has both a cultural and individual component, is tied to other emotions, links people, and reduces fear.

As a change leader, you're working with people – and people are driven by emotion. It's contagious, it's instant, it's irrational... but it's also understandable. Paying attention to neuroscience provides invaluable clues and sets key priorities for our work.

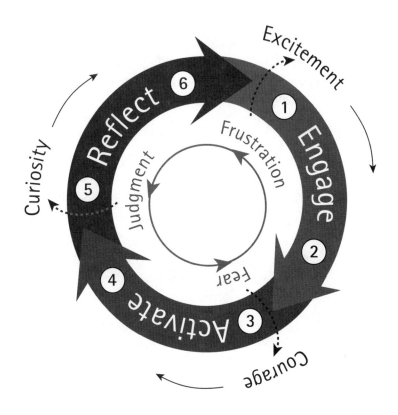

Part II

The Change MAP

In the next three chapters you'll learn about the phases of the Change MAP in detail. We'll consider the goal of each phase and the emotional transition – then we'll explain the steps and milestones. By the end you'll have a clear picture of every part of the model.

Then, in each chapter you'll find an "Operational Manual" with an explanation of each of 16 actions we recommend for each phase; these can be used as a step-by-step implementation plan, or adapted to meet the unique needs of your change. Finally, at the end of each chapter is a quick recap of the phase.

Phase: **Engage**

Goal: Buy-in to a plan

Transition: Frustration to Excitement

Chapter 4: Engage

The Goal:

The key goal of the "Engage" phase is to get buy-in to a plan. Our assumption here is that the change is not going to proceed on its own – to some degree the wheel is stuck in the mud, and there is some wish to get things moving. Because the Change Map is an iterative process, you don't need to get it completely unstuck right away, you don't need to get "total agreement" nor "the perfect plan," but enough forward momentum and enough clarity that you can begin to move. Each time you cycle through this phase, you will increase the level of clarity and buy-in like an expanding fractal. Start small, keep it simple, and ramp up.

Beneath the Water:

At an emotional level, when change isn't happening, but is needed, people feel some mix of helplessness, fear, and anger. They don't like the status quo, but there are some aspects of it they **do** like, there's something comfortable about it, and the change brings uncertainty. Typically change has started and failed (or not fully succeeded) many times; frustration is the natural result. However, in frustration people will tend to move into defense or attack, so they won't do their best collaborative, creative problem solving. So the "EQ work" is to move yourself and others from "very frustrated and stuck" toward "excited and fully committed." That's a big journey, but you don't need to accomplish it all at once. The first time through you might make a big step just to get to a feeling of "a little frustrated and doubtful – but willing to consider alternatives."

In a typical change process, a small group of people considers the tactical needs of an organization; the group makes plans behind closed doors, then attempts to roll those plans out. To get people on board with the plan, advocates of this methodology say "create a sense of urgency" so people take the change seriously. Yet we know that at an emotional level, "urgency" and "fear" are close cousins, and fear blocks change. We also know that the best companies change not just because of problems, but even more when performance is fairly high, so the fear-based "urgency" won't be effective in this setting. Ideally, we want managers looking forward – not just reacting to the latest crisis (when often it's actually too late). Finally, fear is a short-term motivator. So we need a more substantive, lasting, forward-looking way to motivate people though ongoing change.

Transition: Frustration to Excitement

Later in this chapter, we will outline a series of action in an "operative manual" for this phase. These actions could be done in a mechanistic, "because they told me to" way – that's guaranteed to fail! Your real work isn't to check off the steps, but to move the change. The actions nudge people toward the milestones, the milestones build toward the steps – and it all builds toward the goal, in this case, Buy-In to a Plan. But remember the EQ Change MAP isn't just about the goals, it's also about the transitions – the emotional dynamics that actually drive the success or failure of the process.

The "EQ work" of this phase is the transition from frustration toward excitement. For a deeper understanding of this transition, let's first revisit the Cycle of Resistance. Resistance is natural and beneficial. Resistance prevents us from acting without evaluation and it protects us. We feel resistance when we are pushed beyond our comfort. When we perceive threat, our emotional centers activate moving us into "battle mode," we get ready to fight, flee, or freeze (high). As the sense of pressure (threat) increases, the battle-mode escalates. The more we feel pushed the more we resist – it's a basic rule of emotions.

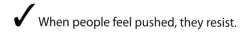 When people feel pushed, they resist.

So how do we move out of resistance?

While it may be possible to "push past" resistance by force, that's very inefficient because as the pressure mounts, so does the resistance. Yet many of us "automatically" react to resistance with increased force. We've developed a habit of it – we push a little, someone pushes back, we push harder… and eventually we're in a shoving match. Maybe psychological, maybe intellectual – but still a power struggle where one will be victor and the other vanquished.

The typical "shoving" strategies are to use facts or threats:

> Facts: "If you had the big picture view, there'd be no question but to go along with the change. Let's just look at the current cash flow…"

> Threats: "If we don't change, we'll all be out of a job…"

Facts don't work in these situations because they're presented with an implicit power grab: "I know the right answer, you don't!" People are not in resistance because of logic – it's an emotional response. So logical solutions will rarely shift the emotional dynamic.

Threats don't work because they just escalate the conflict pushing each party further into "being right." It is important to notice when we're threatening in subtle ways – for example by presenting "facts" about the dire consequences of someone not doing what we want them to do.

On the other hand, sometimes we give information and "push" people in a positive way. While it may appear to be a grey area, it's actually a simple matter to distinguish between the two: When we are trying to control others, we attempt to take power and make ourselves right OVER them; when we are supporting others, we give them power. We'll talk more about power in part three, but it's an important dimension to consider as you consider the Change MAP process.

Remember, **how** you do the actions has a dramatic effect. In other words: You can do all the right things, but if you do them in the wrong ways you won't get positive results. Because emotions are such a critical component in change, your attitude and intention are just as important as the action steps to follow.

Defining Terms

This transition is from frustration toward excitement. What do those words mean?

Excitement is a feeling that blends anticipation, the emotion of "looking forward," with joy, the emotion of "wishes met." Excitement occurs when people connect with a possibility that is important to them and when there is some path that's likely to produce positive effects; it energizes people to move toward that potential.

The basic message of excitement is that bright possibilities are coming. As people move toward that potential (or perceive that they're moving), the feeling intensifies. This fuels forward momentum.

On the other hand, people feel **frustrated** when they are stuck and want to move forward, but they're not getting the results they want. Frustration is a form of anger – anger is the emotion that arises when your way is blocked. If you want to get to a meeting and the car won't start, you get angry at the car for not working (or maybe your friend for not refilling the gas tank…). The anger focuses your attention on the obstacle.

Frustration is more generalized. It comes when there are many sources of anger building up over time, hemming you in, blocking your progress. Because there's no clear obstacle, you can't focus your energy to push through the block, and frustration simmers.

The basic message of frustration is, "things aren't going the way I want," and as the situation continues, other "stuck" feelings grow – such as disappointment (tried and failed), helplessness (nothing else I can do), shame (I am bad), blame (someone else is bad).

Have you ever had the experience of feeling frustrated and moving from there to "slightly annoyed" to "maybe possible" to "can do" then into positive action? Remembering these experiences will help you develop insight into doing so again, and supporting others to make the emotional transition.

What was the situation?

What was frustrating?

Did someone help you make the change? What are some of the characteristics and qualities s/he brought to help you?

Did you have a way to express your frustration and "feel heard"?

When you expressed your frustration, what were some new insights or feelings that helped?

What were some action steps you took?

What can you distill from this experience to use in the future?

Your own experience of moving past frustration is a great place to start a deeper inquiry into this emotional dynamic, but remember: People are strange. We mean that in a loving way – strange and fascinating! There are some fundamental similarities – we work with all kinds of people, all over the world, and the basic emotional dynamics are consistent. However, each person comes to the room each day with his own filters, experiences, assumptions, awareness, personality, and competencies. So it's best to treat each situation as new:

 While others are a lot like you, it's virtually guaranteed that their reactions will be different.

Watch Out

One way of planning this transition is to consider typical "hot buttons" that increase frustration:

Excluding: When people feel left out, isolated, or ignored

Contradicting: When people perceive their ideas are

being dismissed without due consideration

Blaming: When people feel accused or attacked

Remember that in the emotional realm, facts are not so important. You might perceive that on a "purely logical" level, someone isn't being excluded, contradicted, or blamed – but people are not purely logical. The question is, do they FEEL excluded, contradicted, or blamed? What's triggering those feelings?

Sometimes they create the feelings themselves. Some people just want to be miserable, and they fabricate all kinds of unpleasant stench. But most people don't. So start by assuming that the people you're working with want to be on board, they want to have a thriving workplace, they want to be part of the solution. What might they be experiencing, seeing, or hearing that's fueling their frustration?

Consider

One of the most powerful tools for facilitating others' transition is your own emotion. Emotions are contagious; at a neurobiological level we are wired to scan the "pack" and assess others' emotional states. We have specific brain centers, and a system of brain cells called "mirror neurons" that work to tune into others' feelings. Others' expressions and actions are mapped into our brains – our mirror neurons are firing to give us a visceral sense of what's happening in others. This system makes people highly attuned to others' emotions – and there is a crossover effect: we have feelings about our perceptions of others' feelings.

 The first step to leading the transition is to Navigate your own emotions.

Breaking down the process:

Phase: **Engage**

2 Steps:

- Enroll People
- Feel the Vision

4 Milestones:

- Understand the Drivers
- Create Hope
- Draft the Map
- Invite to change

16 Actions suggested in the Operational Manual

Engage | Steps and Milestones

In order to move change forward, we need "IQ plus EQ." It's essential to make a plan that will be effective at the tactical level and will reach the appropriate return on investment. At the same time, we need a plan that will work – and people will need to make it work.

So in this phase, you're working to blend head and heart – to gain a clear understanding of the current context, the new opportunity, and the drivers of the status quo (what's keeping you where you are). At the same time, you're doing the "people work" to build positive momentum.

To do so, there are two key steps – the first more focused on the current reality, the second more focused on the path forward. Within each objective are two key milestones. Later in the chapter we'll discuss a variety of action steps that can be used to reach each milestone.

Steps and Milestones in the Engage Phase:

1. Enroll People: Bring people into the possibility of change

> Understand the Drivers: Increase insight into the current status, tactically and emotionally

> Create Hope: Create an emotional shift to begin galvanizing people

2. Feel the Vision: Clarify direction and build commitment

> Draft the Map: Craft an initial plan that's measurable, valuable, and simple

Invite to Change: Give people the opportunity to be part of the change

The way you will achieve each milestone will vary depending on the specific situation and where you are in the cycle of change. If you're on your first iteration through the cycle, you might choose certain actions that are different from the fifth time through – but we'll suggest four actions for each milestone, a kind of "cookbook" that you can use prepare a feast of change.

Step 1: Enroll People

Engagement is crucial. When we are involved in a decision, we are more committed to the outcome. A classic experiment illustrates this truth: Half the group was randomly assigned with a lottery ticket number, the other half was asked to create their own lottery number. Before the winning numbers were revealed, researchers asked members of both groups to sell their tickets. The researchers needed to pay five times more to buy the self-created numbers – irrespective of age and other factors. This is the power of involvement. If you want five times the commitment, involve people in the process.

Frequently clients have told us that they don't want to make change more complex by involving more people in the discussion. Fair enough – it certainly would be easier if you could just tell people to change... but it doesn't seem to work. On the other hand, if you use the change process as an opportunity for people to take ownership of the future, not only will the change be more effective, at the end you'll have a higher level of commitment, trust, and accountability.

One absolutely critical resource in this phase is clarity of values and principles. As you're beginning to plot the course of the change process and bringing people into the conversation, the plan will go awry without and ethical rudder. As we'll discuss many times in the book, purpose is at the center of the change process, and the change must be linked to purpose. In turn, purpose must aligned with individual and organizational values. To continue the ship metaphor, this lets the wind, sails, compass, rudder and crew all work toward same direction.

To be effective in this phase, equip yourself with an abundance of emotional intelligence (or "EQ" for "emotional quotient"). Your EQ will help you see and understand what's happening at a human level, and to help others see that too. What are the pros and cons of the current situation? What do people feel now? What do people want to feel? What's holding you back, what's pushing you forward? Where can you find the energy to make a step up?

Vision is one of the most powerful tools in this process. A powerful vision is not only a statement, but a living idea that is compelling both intellectually and emotionally. Many companies are working only on what needs fixing, but the energy to do so comes when we see what is possible. There are many kinds of visions – some focused on EBIT and ROI, some focused on being the best, some on adding value and meaning in the world – different visions motivate different people differently. It's critical to understand the people involved in this change and what matters to them. So the first milestone is to **Understand the Drivers**.

1.1 Understand the Drivers

There are many ways to approach this milestone. The goal is to have a clear picture of the current reality. Who is involved, why are they here, what do they want and need, what will move them, etc. Here are four recommended actions, which we'll explain in more detail:

1. **Work WITH human nature** (ground your planning in reality by tapping into the latest neuroscience to gain a clear picture of what drives people)

2. **Listen responsively** (gather data and let people "feel heard." Understand the stories that are shaping the culture; where is the power, where is the frustration, where is the hope?)

3. **Check the vital signs** (get a clear picture of what the current emotional reality and the deeper motivators at work)

4. **Craft a new story** (begin to create "emotional alchemy" beginning to transform the emotional state from frustration toward excitement)

Generally these four actions will take several days of focused work for a relatively simple change, and as much a two-three weeks for a more complex change.

Again, as you make the action plan around this milestone, remember that HOW you do these actions will contribute to, even control, the results. For example, imagine that someone "listens" while they're full of impatience and frustration versus someone who listens with genuine curiosity and compassion. How would each affect the emotional climate? How would the listener's attitude change the data they received? So as you work on this milestone, remember your larger objective – to increase understanding – and goal – to enroll people.

1.2 Create Hope

The second milestone is to **Create Hope**. As we discussed in

Part One, people come into a new change carrying the baggage of many past failures. They feel stuck, and even if there is compelling logic, the feelings of distrust and doubt pervade. Why? Because, you don't change feelings with logic. Feelings are, by definition, not rational!

Hope is a feeling that arises when you see a possibility of getting what you want. It focuses you on the opportunity and creates energy to move toward that potential. The opposite, hopelessness, is "knowing" that there is no path forward. Where hopelessness is an experience of resignation, hope is one of potential. It isn't a certainty – we only feel hope when there is challenge and uncertainty, but it's the critical ingredient that moves us to stand up and "play the match."

At the same time, real hope comes not from faith, but from credence. Hope requires a path forward. Then when the path solidifies into a real plan, hope solidifies into optimism and commitment. So when you work to create hope, you need to connect at an emotional level while also providing a trustworthy, credible opportunity to move the situation forward.

To reach this milestone, we typically use these four actions:

1. **Assess and navigate your own emotions** (identify and learn from your feelings, then transform them to serve you rather than visa versa)

2. **Announce change** (begin forming a group of people to support the possibility of change, not an explicit plan but a "yes we can" intention)

3. **Acknowledge, validate, accept feelings** (recognize that there will be a variety of reactions and accept those; do not hide from the difficulty and complexity, but likewise do not be daunted when people act like people)

4. **Connect to purpose** (re-state why this is actually important and help people see that together we're doing something that matters)

All of these actions can occur in one day – such as preparing for then having a meeting of key stakeholders.

Step 2. Feel the Vision

If you have successfully brought your change to this point, you've moved from "completely stuck" to "open to move." Maybe there's not real action, there's probably not firm commitment – but there's potential. The next step is to build on this openness to create an initial plan. "Feel" the vision rather than "See" the vision because it's not enough to have a pretty chart with lots of tables and arrows. We need to build on the initial enrollment and move toward real buy-in.

You also have to be careful to have just enough of a plan. Too much planning will bog you down. Too little will leave you unprepared. Remember this is a "Ready, Fire, Aim" process. We're working on the "Ready" stage, and that means we need SOME clarity. The first time through the cycle, maybe it's very little. The 10th time through, we probably have a very detailed project plan.

2.1 Draft the Map

We use the term "Draft" because it's a work in process. As soon as you and others perceive this to be a fixed document, it's not worth much. It can be powerful to make a beautifully drawn map, it can be useful to create extensive tables and charts – but the essence of the map is a vision of moving from the current reality to the desired state, and by definition that will evolve rapidly. So don't get too attached.

Working on the **Draft the Map** milestone you will develop a coalition of allies who will guide and drive the change with you, and together you'll articulate the vision and key steps. It's important to develop around the end-state: What will success look like? How will you know you've succeeded? What numbers will change? How can you track it along the way?

Then you'll begin sharing that with a wider circle (especially for larger-scale change, such as organizational change) and including more and more people as co-owners of the change. Then, in the next milestone, you'll move people to commitment.

Here are four actions to consider:

1. **Identify supporters who will build excitement** (create a team of change designers and leaders)

2. **Create a plan** (articulate the goal and some key steps)

3. **Define metrics and milestones** (identify ways to measure progress)

4. **Gather feedback, co-create, refine** (expand the circle to increase ownership)

Generally these actions occur over one to three weeks. Dragging it out is dangerous, as is shortcutting. Depending on the complexity of the change and where you are on the spiral, you might do all these in a couple of meetings with a key group, or you might need to schedule a series of committee meetings and focus group sessions followed by "lunch and learn" type discussions for the fourth step.

2.2 Invite to Change

It's now time to move to commitment and call for buy-in to the plan with the second milestone in step 2: **Invite to Change**. This is an invitation, not a mandate – if you've done the ground-work, then participation will be seen as an opportunity to be part of the solution, and the "right" people (including you!) will say Yes!

We recommend these actions in pursuit of the "Invite to Change" milestone:

1. **Share the plan** (ask: do you want to be part of it?)

2. **Apply Consequential Thinking** (help people evaluate costs and benefits)

3. **Give ownership** (remind them: you are needed, you have a role)

4. **Clarify commitment** (define roles and expectations, tactically and emotionally)

It's likely you'll conduct all four of these steps in one meeting (or for large groups, in a series of meetings).

Operational Manual

In this section you will find 16 actions to facilitate the Engage phase. You may not use all of these in every change – consider this a "menu" of tools to help you reach each milestone.

Step 1: Enroll People |
Milestone 1: Understand the Drivers

1.1.1 Work WITH neuroscience

As you prepare for your change adventure, start by refreshing your understanding of "what makes people tick." This helps you enter into the process with curiosity – as a learner engaged in a laboratory of discovery. Starting from this context, you have a much higher likelihood of success, first because you will listen and understand more accurately, and second because you will be more resilient and flexible in the face of the inevitable set-backs. In Part 1, Chapter 3, you read about several principles of neuroscience and emotion, here is a quick recap of three key points:

- Engagement is based on deep motivators. As you consider the current change, how engaged are the people involved? How does this change connect with deep motivators? How can you add meaning and depth to connect to these core drivers?

- You cannot force people to change. You can inspire them, you can create meaning, but you cannot change people. Choice is the key to move people. Can you transform "The Change" in "**Our** Change"? Remember that certain emotions are signals to protect/defend/attack and cause a narrowing of focus, while others create forward momentum toward opportunity – for example excitement, hope, trust, curiosity, joy, caring, and wonder are all "expansive" feelings. How can you fuel and tap those?

- Emotions are not logical. You work with emotions at an emotional level, not through being right and having the rational plan. Even when the emotion is based on "wrong facts," the emotion is real.

✓ Perception is more real than the reality.

1.1.2 Listen responsively

Presumably you are reading this book because you want to make change. Whether that's a personal, team, or organizational change, it's valuable to recognize that the current situation has taken time to evolve. You have arrived at this point "loaded" -- the canvas is not blank. You, your team, and your organization are carrying the experiences, learnings, assumptions, culture, systems, and feelings from all that has come before. Some of that is invaluable, some is neutral, and some is in the way, and it's very difficult to know which fits in which category!

To add to the complexity, each person is carrying something different because each has arrived at today through different experiences, hearing different stories, learning different lessons – and with different competencies.

Thus, today you, your team, and your organization sit with some level of chaos. Perhaps you have an overall vision of where to go next, and perhaps some urgency to change because the "status quo" isn't ideal. At the same time there are different views, different pictures of the current situation and how to move forward. Often there are competing agendas, and often, different people and groups are assigning blame for what's not working in the status quo.

Consider a change you are seeking to implement with a team.

- How many different views are there of the current situation? What are some of those views?

- Are some people assigning blame for the current situation? Are people blaming one another?

- To what extent is there "common ground," a shared picture of the present situation?

- To what extent is there common vision, a shared picture of the desired goal?

To accurately answer these questions you'll need to hone your emotional intelligence to see both the "tactical" level and the underlying human dynamics. Emotional intelligence, or EQ, allows you to integrate your thinking and feeling to make optimal decisions about yourself and others. This intelligence is essential for you as Change Leader to be effective at the people-side of the process.

Typically when we begin working with a team or organization, we start to listen to the different perspectives, not assessing who is "right" and who is "wrong," but facilitating the team to discover their common ground.

We were launching a change project with a health care organization. After meeting with the CEO and COO and talking with the Chairman, we heard there were strongly entrenched cultural differences between different units and a lot of blame – in the face of serious business pressures (too much debt, loss of key staff, declining reputation) the leadership was not willing to come together to solve their problems. Our next step was to facilitate a session with the CEOs of eight different business units plus several of the key people from the corporate office. One of the first activities was to ask each person to make a symbolic representation of their vision: "If everything goes well in the next 18 months, how will the organization look?" It was fascinating that despite the rancor, almost every person used similar symbols and metaphors in their vision. We didn't even have to point it out – they immediately began to talk about the commonalities in their vision. This shared perspective didn't solve the problem, but it opened the door to have a more serious conversation about the path forward.

 When people "feel heard," they are more open to the plan

1.1.3 Check the vital signs

When you are admitted to a hospital, your vital signs are checked – blood pressure, heart beat, breathing rate, and temperature – to monitor your physical functioning. Likewise, we can consider the vital signs for organizational functioning, and for the individual's, and team's, ability to function within the organization.

At the organizational level, we use these six parameters:

Climate Factor	Definition
Alignment	To what extent are people involved in their organization's stated mission and the execution thereof? Do they feel a sense of belonging to the organization?

Accountability	To what extent do people in the organization see themselves and others following through on commitments? Are they motivated and do they take responsibility for their choices and the outcomes?
Collaboration	How well do people interact with one another and share information? Do they work and solve problems together?
Leadership	What level of commitment do employees have to their leaders? How do they perceive their leaders and leadership throughout the organization? Are people capable, competent, and worth following?
Adaptability	Are people seeking change? Are they ready to adapt? Are they flexible problem-solvers and open to innovation?
Trust	Do people have a sense of faith and belief in the organization and its leaders? Can people rely on the integrity of others? Do they have confidence in others' abilities and intentions?

You can use the Organizational Vital Signs assessment, or some other method, to check these areas. Your goal is to understand the current emotional reality at an organizational or systemic level so that as you move to enroll people, you are working for a clear understanding of "what is."

In parallel, it's important to understand where you and other key players are emotionally. We've created a simple Engagement Vital Signs metric based on the Motivation Iceberg model we explained in Part III, Chapter 3; use this tool to track your emotional engagement. Because these feelings drive those deeper motivations, Engagement Vital Signs (EVS) tells you how much capacity you and others have to drive change. Try it:

How are you feeling now? Circle one number per row...

Unsafe	1	2	3	4	5	Safe
Stagnant	1	2	3	4	5	Developing
Flailing	1	2	3	4	5	Accomplishing
Isolated	1	2	3	4	5	Belonging
Meaningless	1	2	3	4	5	Purposeful

Looking above and summarizing, how do you feel globally?

Disengaged	1	2	3	4	5	Engaged

We suggest tracking this metric regularly. Sometimes it will go up or down because of factors you're aware of and managing (e.g., after having a challenging conversation), but if you're seeing unexpected changes, or if the barometer falls overall, that's time for some EQ intervention (see Part III). On page 115 we will talk more about metrics to track change.

1.1.4 Craft a new story

Working on the next milestone you will begin to communicate about the change. You'll need a story to tell – one that acknowledges the challenge and frustration while beginning to shift the emotional reality toward hope and possibility. When we say "story" we mean "a way of explaining" or "a narrative of the situation."

A good story has a beginning, middle, and an end. The beginning sets the context, the middle includes challenge, and the end acknowledges growth and change.

Your first "audience" for this story is yourself. How are you talking to yourself about this change? Notice the words you use and the implicit emotional message and power in those words. We use this model of "Victim-Dictator-Ally" language to help with that assessment.

Domain	Victim	Dictator	Ally
Sample Words	I can't... They're making me... I have to...	You should... You have to... There's no choice...	We can... I wonder if... How could we...
Dynamics	Gives up power, makes others responsible	Takes power, makes others dependent	Shares power, fosters interdependence

Your study of the current situation and the emotional reality are essential for putting together an effective story about the change. The story helps you and others see the change honestly + optimistically – there is challenge and opportunity.

Step 1: Enroll People | Milestone 2: Create Hope

1.2.1 Assess and navigate your own emotions

In Part III we'll share more specific tools for "Navigating Emotions," here is a brief summary:

The nature of emotions is to flow and change – emotions are made of small chains of protein produced in the brain and in the body. A kind of neurohormone, the molecules of emotion course through our blood reaching and regulating every cell. They function as part of our regulatory system, focusing attention and activating our bodies to respond to the environment. Literally emotions are information (chemically encoded signals) and energy (electro-chemical capacity). The chemicals are released in "bursts" or "cascades" flowing back and forth forming a kind of feedback loop between brain and body (and between people). Each "burst" lasts for about six seconds, and then the chemicals are absorbed and recycled. In addition to our own feelings, our brains and bodies are attuned to pick up signals from others. At any given time we'll have at least several different types of these chemicals flowing though us producing a complex and flavorful "stew" that we experience.

To a large degree we have choice about how we feel. The initial burst of chemicals is an automatic, conditioned response to stimulus. Then the cascade (of follow-on bursts) is affected by our thoughts, perceptions, and actions. The underlying conditioning, or "rules" defining how to respond, is partly learned and partly innate. For example, when you taste something nasty, you're innately wired to experience the feeling of disgust, but you learn to what degree and how it's appropriate to express (show) that. At the same time, you have multiple feelings, and you have a great deal of volition about which of those feelings to emphasize by "leaning in" or paying attention to them. We also are able to "synthetically" create feelings – for example, if you smile and laugh (for no "real" reason whatsoever) you will produce the SAME "happy molecules" as if you were "genuinely" happy.

When we talk about "Navigating Emotions," we're suggesting a balance between engaging in and managing your feelings. At one end is wallowing in feelings and letting them run amok, at the other is repressing or dominating feelings through force of will – if you remember the old Star Trek, Doctor "Bones" McCoy could represent the "feelings rule" end of the spectrum, and the Vulcan Mr. Spock represents the other extreme. Neither, by itself, is an effective use of emotion. Navigating Emotion represents a middle ground where you work with and through emotion to gain insight and to move yourself and others in a worthwhile direction.

As you'll read in Part III, Tools for Emotions, the basic rule for Navigating Emotions is to validate feelings. Rather than denying, or saying "I shouldn't feel this," or "it's bad for me to…," face the information in a factual manner: You have these feelings. What are they telling you? One of the most powerful ways of engaging in this inquiry is to say (and feel) to yourself, "Isn't that interesting?"[54]

In part 1.1.2, above, we asked you to consider a situation and other people's perspectives. Now consider yourself in the situation:

- What is your view of the situation?

- How do you feel now?

- How are your feelings affecting the way you see the situation?

- What are those feelings telling you – how are they "trying to help" you? *

- How do you **want** to feel, and how would that help you?

- Do you have ANY of those feelings you want to have? Can you "lean in" and emphasize those?

Note that until you validate and explore your current feelings it is almost impossible to Navigate to new feelings. Consider that the current feelings are there for an important reason – they won't go away until their message is delivered.[55]

---

* Remember, feelings are primal – that means they are working to ensure safety and survival. If in doubt about the purpose of a feeling, consider: What is this protecting?

Recognizing and transforming your own emotions is an excellent way to develop the skills you'll need working with others. In addition, because emotions are contagious, and because emotions affect the way people think and interact, your emotional state in this process is pivotal.

 Your own emotions are one of the most powerful tools you have for shifting others' emotions.

Once you've taken stock of your own emotional state and navigated your way to readiness, it's time to move forward engaging others and building the shared vision.

1.2.2 Announce change

At this stage you're working on creating hope to enroll people. So do not craft your announcement of change as a complete plan, nor as a logical treatise, nor as a "change or die" dire warning, but as an opportunity to move toward a better future. At the same time, you don't want to downplay the seriousness of the current situation or you lose credibility. In essence, the message is:

"The current situation isn't good enough – we need to make change for the better."

Unfortunately there's not a "perfect" way to do this – you need authenticity and clarity of mind and conviction. A great example is Barack Obama's speech at 2004 DNC Convention almost three years before he became a candidate for president. After acknowledging the difficultires, both at an intellectual and emotional level, Obama turned to hope:

> "It's the hope of slaves sitting around a fire singing freedom songs. The hope of immigrants setting out for distant shores. The hope of a young naval lieutenant bravely patrolling the Mekong Delta. The hope of a mill worker's son who dares to defy the odds. The hope of a skinny kid with a funny name who believes that America has a place for him, too.
>
> Hope! Hope in the face of difficulty! Hope in the face of uncertainty! The audacity of hope! In the end, that is God's greatest gift to us, the bedrock of this nation. A belief in things not seen. A belief that there are better days ahead."*

What's intriguing about the Obama case is that the majority of his campaign focused on the "Yes we can" attitude – not on facts, force and fear, but on possibility. In fact, he was often criticized for not having a clear plan. This strategy exemplifies the notion that buy-in comes when people participate in the planning.

At a personal level, this announcement of change might be informing supporters: I've decided to change, I don't know exactly how, but ___ is going to be different.

At team and organizational levels it's similar, and often an opportunity to begin to ask: "Who wants to be part of the planning?"

One of our clients, Luigi Boaretto at CIBA Specialty Chemicals in Bologna, used this process in announcing a major restructuring including a significant reduction in workforce. After going through many of the actions above, his basic message to

---

* Here is the keynote on YouTube:
http://www.youtube.com/watch?v=eWynt87PaJ0

his senior leadership team: The company has given this plant a mandate to change, we don't have choice about that. Then, after time for acknowledging, validating, and accepting feelings (action 1.2.3), Luigi went on to the next step, connecting to purpose, and inviting his team to be part of the solution.

In essence he said: This is terrible, and while it feels like we're being forced, we do have choice – we can be the ones who drive the change or we can be the victims. If we drive the change, then we have the opportunity to protect and grow what's most important to us here. Who wants to be part of that?

1.2.3 Acknowledge, validate, accept feelings

As you can imagine in Luigi's example, above, after an announcement of change, there will be a lot of different feelings. Many of them will be… strong. A common response is to try to quickly move away from those feelings – it's uncomfortable for most of us to experience a lot of dissent, pain, and frustration. But moving away from it is unlikely to make it go away.

As with Navigating your own emotions, the critical step here is to acknowledge feelings and not run from them. Acknowledging means noticing versus denying, which is a great starting point, but in itself not enough. Validating means confirming or making official, which is deeper. Accepting means "considering or holding as true," which is even deeper. When we move toward acceptance we're deeply valuing people's experience and this sends a powerful message.

It's tough because these feelings are often uncomfortable, and someone's disappointment, fear, and anger can easily be taken as a personal attack, especially if you're in a position of power. It's as if you're failing. But at the same time, when people are willing to express their feelings, they're showing you trust and commitment. Apathy is the enemy of engagement – strong feelings only occur when there is a lot at stake.

Tom Wojick, a consultant in our network, told us a story of a school superintendent who had to announce the closure of a school. Her first plan was to structure the meeting in such as way as to minimize the opportunity for the participants to talk so the "unpleasant feelings wouldn't get out of control." With Tom's help, she took a radically different approach. She made the announcement of change, then empathically and honestly walked the audience through the emotions she experienced in this process, from shock to disappointment to despair to anger, often connecting with them, for example saying, "I imagine many of you feel this too." Then she continued the emotional journey explaining how she began to reconnect with purpose, and how her vision of the district hasn't changed. In this phase she spoke about moving toward what's most important – and invited people to be part of that. Then she asked them to work in small groups to discuss their perceptions of the situation, and if and how they would like to be part of the next phase of growth.

1.2.4 Connect to purpose

In all three examples of announcing change that we've just shared – Boretto's, Obama's, and the superintendent's, the message began with a confrontation of reality, moved to a validation of feelings, and then expanded to a reconnection to deeper purpose.

As we discussed in Part I, Chapter 3, purpose is one of the deepest of human motivators. It's obvious this way – which of these two are you more likely to accept?

> "I want you to work harder, dig deeper, and give me extra commitment so our shareholders can make more profit."

> "I want you to endure struggle and sacrifice to protect something vitally important."

This process of reconnecting to purpose has a profound emotional effect, so it's one of the key tools for Navigating Emotions. If you don't have a purpose, or can't find how the change you're making serves that purpose, now's a good time to pause and do some serious work.

 You will not drive significant change unless it serves a significant purpose.

Step 2. Feel the Vision | Milestone 1: Draft the Map

2.1.1 Identify supporters who will build excitement

You started this process in 1.2.3 when you announced the change in a way that invited people to be part of the solution. Now it's time to formalize that invitation. Perhaps you form a planning committee or a support group. Perhaps you change organizational roles to free up a group's time to devote significant energy to this work.

Then you need to "constitute" the group. This is typically an initial meeting where you "contract": What are we doing together, how will we work together to do that? The role of assent is key here – you want people committed, you need their discretionary effort (i.e., far above and beyond what's "required" by the job).

A few tips working with this group:

> Maintain focus on the larger goal and your shared purpose.

> Hold yourselves as serving that purpose and the larger group (if there is one, e.g., the rest of the team). You're not there to "be in charge," you're there to facilitate.

> Accept frustration, fear, etc, but do not permit yourself or the group to stay there.

> Call one another on breach of the group contract – if you've agreed "no side conversations in our meetings," then be accountable to that.

> Remember that what happens here will be replicated and expanded as the change progresses – it's as important to get the process right as it is to get the product right. As Gandhi said, you will not create peace through violence.

> Pair yourself with positive stimulus – bring treats, spontaneous fun, humor, etc.

Plan these meetings carefully considering: What do you want the group to feel? In a sense, working with this group is like winding the rubber band on a toy airplane. You're building up emotional energy that will fuel the change. The more challenging the change, the more emotional energy you'll need to redirect it.

The energy required to catalyze change is proportional to the energy driving the status quo.

2.1.2 Create a plan

The next step is to focus in on the emerging vision. Before going through the analysis of what is actually viable, keep the door of possibility open. What is exciting? What is powerful? Again, it's essential to craft these ideas together in a way where one input builds on another. This is "common sense," we don't have any particularly world-changing process for building the vision, except that a compelling shared vision will only emerge from a healthy team climate. Emotion is a critical ingredient to the creative process, perhaps it's the fuel, so, in this phase our attention is on shaping a healthy emotional dynamic (see the Transition discussion at the start of this chapter).

What emerges is a shared sense of direction – not a full-fledged plan; rather than a carefully wordsmithed vision-mission-values or strategy document, we're looking for vectors coming together in a common direction. Later it will be important to craft the message carefully in order to enroll more people in this direction.

A useful exercise here is a "Quest Map." Basically, we provide a blank paper and colored markers and ask people to draw a map showing the pathway from their current state to their goal. This can be done individually and combined, but combining can be challenging, so experiment with doing one together. Try one yourself now; the map could include:

- Where are you?

- Where do you want to go?

- Who are some of the people involved in this process?

- What are some of the feelings it's important to create on this journey?

- What are some of the key "highlights" on the way (events, accomplishments)?

Now it's time to become more specific. Depending, again, on where you are in the change spiral, your level of detail will vary. The first time through the cycle you'll see a messy blob in the present, an exciting potential in the future, and the need to define a path from here to there. A few times through the cycle, you'll have spiraled to a much higher level of detail.

As we've discussed, it's not the "complete" plan, perhaps it's the 90-day tactical outline that will move the change forward. The key ingredients of a successful plan are:

> Just Simple Enough - a simplistic approach won't be credible, a "complete" plan won't ever go into effect. The ideal plan is in the middle - built for speed, meaning it will move efficiently, and built for purpose, meaning it will take people toward someplace worth going. The US Navy uses a phrase, "80% solution" -- get moving toward the target and then refine.

> Clear Metrics - so you can track and focus the change and know the level of success; this will become imperative in Phase 3.

> People - a plan is "good" only if your people will come on board to execute it.

2.1.3 Define metrics and milestones

The next action is to refine the plan with specific outcomes and a way to track your progress. Consider:

- What will success look like?

- Where will you be in 90 days? 60? 30? 10? 5? Tomorrow?

- What are some ways of tracking that progress?

- Is there an existing metric that you track that can be used? If not, what will effectively reflect success in this process?

Ideal metrics are easy and clear. You can use sophisticated tools – we publish several – but you can also do this manually. It's also important to choose metrics that are likely to change if you're on track. Some metrics, such as sales volume, can be slow to change and are highly susceptible to external factors. Others, such as overtime, are much more under your direct influence. For example:

- Suppose you're working on a team change to increase collaboration. Put a white board in the meeting room. Every time someone perceives splintering in the group, they put a tick on the whiteboard. Add up the ticks every week.

- Perhaps you're making a personal change to increase your health. Put on a pedometer. Write down the number of steps you take each week.

- Imagine you're leading an effort to build a more productive workplace climate. Count up the number of incidents, accidents, and complaints each week.

There are several reasons for spending time to identify the right metrics. One, of course, is so you can assess the efficacy of the strategies you employ in Phase Two. But a more subtle reason is that by simply focusing on the metric, you put attention there. You have to be careful though – for example, standardized tests used in many educational systems actually reduce learning because they "dumb down" intellectual growth to something easy to measure on a multiple-choice test. Remember:

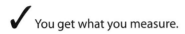 You get what you measure.

With our clients we use a hybrid of their existing business metrics (e.g., customer satisfaction, turnover, percentage of sales quota, waste, overtime, defect rate, market share), invented metrics (e.g., pad of paper by your desk tracking the number of times you get emails or calls blaming others), and our Vital Signs tools. The Vital Signs tools help us maintain focus on the people-side of the process. Because they are statistically validated, rigorous assessments, we have a fairly strong sense that the tools measure what's important. Depending on the project, we choose from a range of our commercial products and custom-made assessments. The SEI tools focus on emotional intelligence as it applies to performance. The Vitals Signs tools provide rapid updates to the leader's dashboard to continually calibrate implementation.

Here's an overview of the tools we've developed to support change[*]:

SEI: Six Seconds Emotional Intelligence Assessment measures eight key competencies that drive the people-side of leadership; these are put in context of critical work and life outcomes.

---

[*] These tools have been researched and developed over the course of a decade by Six Seconds' researchers and practitioners world-wide. Information on the commercially available tools is on www.6seconds.org/tools/

We use this tool when it's important to develop peoples' skills with people and emotions, for example those who need to create a healthy organizational culture or manage people through complex situations (including change).

SEI 360: Six Seconds Emotional Performance Feedback tool tracks the effect of EQ – how people are performing on an emotional level. The flexible 360 platform allows us to define any variation of different groups from which an individual receives feedback. We use this tool when it's important to understand the way individuals are affecting one another, for example in leadership teams.

TVS: Team Vital Signs allows the group to assess the team dynamics and relationships as a whole in six key aspects of the climate (gut feel) including trust. TVS is a variation of OVS, below, and can be used in parallel or when working only at the team level. We use this when teams need to become more functional and focused (which is a key issue in change) and to track their improvements.

OVS: Organizational Vital Signs is an automated online (or paper) survey tool that rapidly measures organizational climate and provides comparisons between departments, divisions, sites, etc. We use this on a regular basis in organizational change projects, first to collect data (per action 1.1.2) to focus the strategy, then to track the efficacy of interventions.

EVS: Engagement Vital Signs is an online collection tool for real-time tracking of the key drivers of motivation. Data is aggregated over time for individuals, by teams, and across the organization to put people on the leader's dashboard. We use this to maintain focus on the people-side of change.

CLA: Customer Loyalty Audit is a customizable online tool to measure the key drivers of customer loyalty. It allows comparisons across any combination of segments such as customer type, region, or size – and can also compare internal and external perspectives (e.g., employees vs. customers, or internal vs. external customers). We use this in projects where change needs to focus on improving customer loyalty.

Custom 360: Our 360 feedback platform allows us to rapidly deploy customized 360 assessments that we use when a change project requires individuals to receive feedback about their efficacy in areas not measured by our EQ tools.

Custom Survey: We use customized surveys to explore other aspects of employee and customer opinion, attitude, and behavior when we have projects that require other metrics.

While we certainly recommend these tools and use them ourselves, this isn't a "commercial" for assessments. The point is for you to consider the types of data that will help you focus and track your change process, then collect that information!

2.1.4 Gather feedback, co-create, refine

Once you have the bones of a good plan, it's time to widen the circle. It's very different saying, "I have a plan, what do you think?" (one way feedback) versus saying, "I've got the basics of a plan, would you be willing to work with me to refine it?" (co-creation).

 Participation builds commitment. Commitment builds ownership. Ownership drives change.

This is, in fact, easiest at the beginning of a new spiral of change. People can "come in on the ground floor" and develop a strong sense that the project is "ours." Later, especially in a long spiral, it can be increasingly difficult to make space for more owners. One advantage of the cyclical map is an explicit recognition that you have many opportunities to "start over" with new stakeholders. Just watch the tendency for people to value the open invitation but then say, in essence, "I want to come in and close the door behind me."

For an individual change, the process of gathering feedback, co-creating, refining might mean a series of discussions with your allies - your coach, supervisor, coworker, friend, doctor, uncle, etc. As you discuss your plans with each, keep the "working draft" mentality. One person might have a strong opinion, but he isn't necessarily right – you're working to get the best of all these views.

For a group change, you might have a few, or even many meetings to gather input. Be careful not to spend too much human capital here. This isn't about a perfect plan – it's about gaining clarity and buy-in. The process of discussion is, in itself, a way of moving forward.

You can do this step in a formal way, such as meetings, but often it's more effective do to it at a personal level. For example, if you have a committee planning the change, each one can talk to 10 well-chosen people over the course of a day and gain a lot of valuable ground.

When you've collected data, for example from a survey tool, refer back to that: "People said they wanted to improve collaboration, so the 90-day plan is focused there." This helps "close the loop" for people – you asked, they responded, you heard, and are now prepared to take action on their input. The next step is to invite them to also be part of it.

Step 2. Feel the Vision |
Milestone 2: Invite to Change

2.2.1 Share the plan . . . .

The purpose of this action is to provide information – you've already collected input, now it's time to present the result. "After our discussions last week, here's the decision on next steps."

For most people, the plan will contain few or no surprises; you're re-stating what they've already heard in Step 2.1. So, ideally, it's pretty straightforward, maybe you need to clarify some points, explain why you've chosen one strategy over another, etc.

Two key points:

- Watch defensiveness: You've worked hard to get to this point, and it's natural to feel ownership of this plan. But it's not "your" plan anymore. You're the person pulling it together, so resistance or frustration or doubt about the plan isn't directed at you. One technique is to pass back the challenge:

    Objection: "I just don't see how we can make enough time for this…"

    Response: "That's definitely going to be a challenge. When we ask for commitments, I wonder if you'd consider taking responsibility for ensuring we keep enough time on the calendar…"

- Maintain Work in Process: Remember that the plan is going to be refined in Phase 3. Depending on your project, maybe that's a week, maybe it's 90 days (we suggest that's an outer limit for most plans) – it's time-limited. Hopefully the vision is "right" and when you go to the Reflect phase you'll re-commit to the same vision and just refine, but in any case, this is something to try, something to learn from -- not a "permanent" process. For some people that's frustrating because they want THE answer, and there is a risk of "flip flopping" and not following through to the next iteration of the cycle. But for most people it's reassuring to acknowledge that we're going to do this for a fixed time, then assess and tune it up together.

2.2.2 Apply Consequential Thinking

Before asking for commitment, it's valuable to review. Change has costs. But you're changing for an important reason (right?), so NOT changing also has costs. People may feel that the "staying the same" costs are better because they're known. Or they may want to change, but they don't like the plan – all that is reasonable, so acknowledge it.

Ask forward thinking/feeling questions such as:

- What happens if we don't make this change?
- What happens if we succeed in this change?
- How about if the change goes badly?
- And if it goes well?
- Overall, what are the costs and benefits of pursuing this plan?

Encourage people to think both about themselves and others,

those in the room and out of the room, about the short term and long term, and about both the tactical and emotional levels.*

By "putting it on the table" and recognizing the costs and benefits, you're allowing people to make a real choice.

2.2.3 Give ownership

You've been doing this all along, now it's time to formalize it: "You have a choice – do you want to participate? What role do you want in this change?"

This action applies at the individual level as well, it's about asking yourself: Do I WANT to do this? People don't do things because they should. "Should" is not part of intrinsic motivation. When you are responding "because you should," that's like saying, "I don't want to, but someone else wants me to, so I will..." In other words, the motivation is coming from outside. The risk is, when it gets hard, or when that external motivation gets too far away, you'll stop. As we discuss in the Motivation Iceberg (see Chapter 9), enduring, powerful motivation has to come from inside.

So, when you're moving into the commitment stage, it's not enough to say, "Do this because I want you to." You must find a way for people to experience the change as something they own. Remember, the milestone you are working to reach is "Invite to Change" – there's a huge emotional difference between an "invitation" and a "demand." Even between an "invitation"

---

* Apply Consequential Thinking is one of the core emotional intelligence competencies in the Six Seconds EQ Model; it is the capacity to blend thinking and feeling to evaluate the ramifications of our choices. For more on this, see the chapter "Choose Yourself: Fight or Flow" in *At the Heart of Leadership* by Joshua Freedman and the SEI Assessment.

and a "request." Are you going to be the one pushing every step of this, or are you going to gather the energy and drive from all these people who are going to take the change forward? Unless you have boundless time and energy, the invitation will provide better results.

 This invitation is an opportunity to have a stake in something worthwhile.

We were consulting on a restructure project to a business serving teens who were having trouble. At this point in the change process, we were able to help the whole team look at three options: Continue with the status quo, change, or give up. We helped them look at costs and benefits of each option, and, fortunately, 100% of them agreed change was the best path to meet their purpose. We worked through the "Draft the Map" milestone, then came the challenge: Would they actually take ownership? In a meeting we reviewed the key steps of the transformation plan and asked, "What are you willing to take responsibility for?" Different team members took real ownership of different aspects of the program; they didn't all follow through precisely, and there was a certain chaos is the shared ownership, but there was palpable commitment. The change worked, and that business unit continued to thrive even when the parent company went bankrupt, largely because the staff had real ownership of the program they created.

Frequently when we review Organizational Vital Signs results (the climate assessment) with groups, there is an initial perception that senior leadership needs to make changes to improve the climate. We acknowledge this, but then raise the bar: "If they are willing to work on this, are you willing to work on it too?" Then we go around the room and gather specific, actionable commitments.

Of course there is a risk in giving ownership, because it means giving control. Generally speaking this is a false risk – in fact you are giving up the ILLUSION of control, but still it's uncomfortable.

One more consideration: At this point, the person driving the change (you?) might be much more invested than the others. If this person is a driver and persuader, or just well liked, s/he can "sell" the idea and create a false agreement. People don't want to say no, so they sort of nod their heads, but don't mean it. Maybe 50% commitment is better than 0%... but be real in your understanding: Are they freely and fully saying yes? The next step helps you find out.

2.2.4 Clarify commitment

The final action concludes this milestone as well as this step – and the whole phase. It's "tying the ribbon on the package" to ensure that you're all clear on what's happening and who is doing what.

Sometimes this is as simple as a one-page chart. We often use this action plan tool to summarize the Engage phase, then send it out weekly or monthly in the next phase:

What	Who	When	% Complete
Draft the "Clarify commitment" section	Josh	Dec 28	80%

Of course this is a very simplistic tool, and more complex projects require a more sophisticated tracking mechanism. In the next chapter we'll share Goalkeeper, an online tool for making and meeting goals that is effective for this. There are also many more complex project management tools that can be set up at this point. The point is to get a clear picture: Who has agreed to do what, by when.

It's also worth considering the seriousness and emotional quality of the commitment. Is this a "say yes but we'll wait and see" situation? Is it a "yes because you're making me," or is it a pure and full-voiced "YES"?

Frequently at this point, change leaders are worried that if they don't get a "yes" it will all fall apart and they'll lose the opportunity. That's quite possible. On the other hand, a "fake yes" is worse, because it means the project will fall apart after even more investment has been sunk.

A quick recap

Here are the components of this phase "at a glance":

Phase	Engage			
Goal	Buy-in to a Plan			
Transition	Frustration to Excitement			
Steps	1. Enroll people		2. Feel the Vision	
Milestones	1.1 Understand the Drivers	1.2 Create Hope	2.1 Draft the Map	2.2 Invite to Change
Actions	1.1.1 Work WITH neuroscience 1.1.2 Listen responsively 1.1.3 Check the vital signs 1.1.4 Craft a new story	1.2.1 Assess and navigate your own emotions 1.2.2 Announce change 1.2.3 Acknowledge, validate, accept feelings 1.2.4 Connect to Purpose	2.2.1 Identify supporters who will build excitement 2.2.2 Create a plan 2.2.3 Define metrics and milestones 2.2.4 Gather feedback, co-create, refine	2.2.1 Share the plan 2.2.2 Apply Consequential Thinking 2.2.3 Give ownership 2.2.4 Clarify commitment

Wrapping Up on the Engage Phase

The first time through this phase, you've taken your project from "impossible" to "possible." There's a vision emerging, and some momentum to act. As you cycle through the Change MAP, each time you're in this phase the plan will become more clear, and the commitment will be higher.

Final Thoughts

We call this phase "Engage" because that's the real work. Engagement occurs at both an intellectual-tactical level and at an emotional-experiential level – to engage you need to win heads and hearts, and that takes using both your IQ and your EQ!

Phase: **Activate**

Goal: Experience
Success

Transition: Fear to Courage

Chapter 5: Activate

The Goal:

In essence, pursuing this phase you will learn new ways of operating and then put those in action. It's helpful to maintain a "beginner's mind"[56] and treat this as a learning laboratory – each day is an opportunity for experimentation and observation. As you try out new strategies, techniques, and systems, pay attention to what works. It's not necessary to "get everything right," and attempting to do so will short-circuit your process. When doing something new it's normal and appropriate to have setbacks, meltdowns, total failures… punctuated by moments of progress. Each time you loop through the Change MAP you'll get more and more competent and the new ways will become more fluid.

Beneath the Water:

The experience of learning something new is awkward and uncomfortable, especially for people who are used to being highly competent. As Andre Gide put it:

> One doesn't discover new lands without consenting to lose sight of the shore for a very long time.

However, KNOWING that discomfort is normal doesn't mean it's comfortable! Entering into something new means leaving the comfort of the current situation (even if it's terrible) and going into the unknown. The unknown is scary. That's why trust is so critical in change – trust provides the underlying safety net that facilitates moving forward through fear. This applies to you as an individual, as a team, and in an organization.

Transition: Fear to Courage

When you're not in it, it's easy to minimize the power of fear – it's one of the most powerful survival mechanisms we have, and it's impossible to simply "will it away." However, it is possible to proceed in the face of fear – to acknowledge it, value it, and move forward. That's courage, and building courage will be essential for this phase to be successful.

It's also possible, and valuable, to confront and question fear. Like all emotions, fear isn't rational, and it's easy to let fear fuel itself based on misassumptions. So without denying the reality of the fear, we can consider it and test the assumptions on which the fear is built. This, in itself, is a risk.

Defining Terms

This transition is from fear toward courage. What do those words mean?

Fear tells us that something we care about may be at risk. It is a question provoking us to examine the risks and to test commitment. When we're at the top of the steep ski slope, fear focuses us on the risk and pushes our attention to immovable trees we might crash into. It prompts us to protect, asking us to evaluate the risks and to move away from them.

It's important to note that we don't feel fear if we don't care. It's a message that something we CARE about is at risk, so if we're totally apathetic there's no fear. When we become clear what's at risk, we can then utilize the energy of fear to take care of that. Fear is refined into concern, caring, and commitment.

Another intriguing aspect of fear is that once we're fully committed, the fear goes away. It's like a voice saying, "are you sure?" Once you firmly and fully say, "YES!" the fear subsides. It comes back quickly, though, when you begin to doubt.

Courage is the choice to confront fear – to move forward in the face of fear's demand that you retreat. It's true that you don't have courage unless you have fear – they are part of the same dynamic of moving through a potentially risky situation.

The bigger the perceived risk, the scarier it is. When you feel totally unsafe, you are unlikely to take any risks. But trust is a mediating factor. Fear is tied to a perception of risk and lack of safety, courage is tied to moving forward anyway – and trust tells you which to listen to.

For example: You're standing at the open door of an airplane several thousand feet up, there's nothing between you and the earth except a few clouds. Do you jump? Every fiber of your being says NO! Your heart and mind and body all "know" this is crazy. But you jump. Why?[*]

Because you trust your parachute, you trust yourself, you trust the company that brought you here – or maybe you're just craving that wild adrenalin and love risking your life!

---

[*] By the way, neither of us has done this, so you'll notice we didn't write "we jump" – no way! On a serious note, remember that we only feel fear if we care – so perhaps some people would jump because they don't care that much about the risk.

Taking real risks is nearly impossible when you don't feel safe. Fear, a message of potential-unsafety, will cause the risks to be magnified and the trust to be questioned. On the other hand, trust offers a feeling that you could proceed despite the risk. Whether you trust yourself, your supporters, the change managers, or the situation, trust restores guard rails to a dangerous bridge.

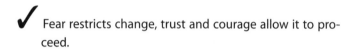 Fear restricts change, trust and courage allow it to proceed.

Again, learning from your own experiences with this transition can help you find insight into the stages of this journey.

- Think of three different times when you felt afraid, uncertain, or anxious. What was that like?

- Can you get yourself to feel those feelings again now?

- Those feelings are telling you: "Something you care about may be at risk." Can you identify the "something you care about" and the risk? The more precisely you identify what's at risk, the more valuable the fear becomes (and generally fear is greater with a more precious risk).

- Did you stay in those feelings, or did they change?

- What helped them change? What did they change into?

- How much courage did you have in those situations? What provided or increased that courage? (Or, what might have helped?)

- In those situations, what/who were you trusting and

not trusting? How did trust affect the fear and courage?

- What are some lessons you can "mine" from this experience about how fear, trust, and courage are related?
About how to move toward courage?

- Check your conclusions with some "emotionally intelligent" colleagues and friends – do they concur with
these conclusions?

For many years the notion seemed to be, if you want courage,
be courageous. True enough. But fortunately there's a growing body of research on courage that can break it down further.
For example, a recent paper from professors at the US Military
Academy found that courage grows from a network of attitudes, skills, support mechanisms, and character traits that can
be strengthened, including:

1. Openness to experience: being willing to try new
   things, experiment, and innovate.

2. Conscientiousness: being committed to accountability
   and follow through.

3. Core self-evaluation: having a forthright self-appraisal
   including a sense of control or self-efficacy (not only
   does the job need to get done, but I will take responsibility for it).[57]

Two more tips about courage:

One way to grow courage is to practice stillness. In difficult conversations don't wiggle, "close" your body language, look away,
etc. – just be present and physically calm. Start this practice
with small risks, you'll find that your own stillness send your
brain and emotions a message that "it's ok," and you'll also begin to send that message to others creating a self-reinforcing,
virtuous spiral.

The second way is to invite it to the party.

✓ Remember in the *Wizard of Oz*, the Cowardly Lion had courage all along. That's probably a universal truth – courage is there, it's a choice to invite it to the surface or leave it buried.

Watch Out

There are many typical "EQ train wrecks" that occur to increase the fear rather than the courage. Avoid these!

- Confusing urgency with fear: When a change is mission critical, you need to take it very seriously. Fear can actually help focus people's attention on the risk. But staying in fear will block adoption and adaptation. Executives often try to create urgency by saying things such as, "if we don't turn this around we won't have jobs next quarter." Fine, sometimes that true – but usually it's presented hyperbolically to "push" the point.

- Communicating from fear: When you are afraid, no matter what you say (and don't say) that fear will transmit. As we discussed in Part One, emotions are contagious, and the most critical emotion to transmit quickly in the "herd" is fear, so we've eons of adaptation to be adept at sensing and transmitting fear.

- Over-focusing on the metric: The metrics are not the real goals, they should help maintain momentum toward the real goal – but they can actually distract and create a false sense of success or failure. Talking too much about the metric narrows vision and increases anxiety.

- Denying the feeling: People who are uncomfortable with "difficult" feelings sometimes pretend those feelings don't exist. You: "I'm uncomfortable with…" Him: "No, don't be ridiculous…" Hmm, do you feel heard? Fear is SERIOUS – it's part of our life-and-death survival system. Take it seriously. Even when the facts don't support the feeling, the feeling is real.

- Closing doors: When a group (team, organization, family, etc.) is in "difficult times," everyone knows it. You're kidding yourself if you think otherwise. But often the patriarchal (and typically male) approach is to go away, shut the door, and privately cope, perhaps making a plan with a couple trusted confederates. "We don't want to worry people." Guess what? When they see a few people going grim faced into your office, they're gonna be plenty worried.

- The hanging axe: One of the most difficult changes for an organization or team is the dreaded RIF (reduction in force). RIF sounds nicer than "firing people," but when people's livelihoods and lives are in the mix, it's painful all around. A frequent failure is doing it slowly. People are left wondering: "When is the axe going to fall? Am I next?" Focus on minimizing the emotional damage, respect all the people in the process (yourself, those losing their jobs, those keeping their jobs), rip the band-aid off quickly, and focus on healing.

Consider

Fear gets a bad rap, but in reality it's a sign of commitment and caring. The problem is that unacknowledged, unprocessed fear grows and gnaws at the spirit. Fear itself can feel dangerous, but it's not. Our reaction to fear can be.

So in these times of uncertainty, respect fear as an advisor and protector – but not as a dictator.

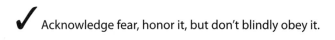 Acknowledge fear, honor it, but don't blindly obey it.

Activate | Steps and Milestones

In this phase you are learning and implementing. The first time through the change cycle maybe you're building and activating new awareness and new attitudes. In the second cycle you're adding new skills. In the third cycle you're beginning to build systems… since it's an ever-adapting, ongoing process, really what you're doing is getting better at learning.

Learning requires unlearning, which is usually the most uncomfortable part. Often when we're starting a consulting project, we'll spend time walking around and "hanging out" with different people in different offices and departments, just asking: "What do you do?" and "Why do you do it this way?" The answers are amazing! We usually hear some variation of "we've always done it this way," sometimes we even hear, "Because it's the law." Unlearning means giving up the comfortable, practiced ways of doing, but also of "being right" and having power. Remember the neuroscience: Unlearning is a conscious process that builds new neural connections in the "executive" area of the brain that serve to redirect the old patterns – the old patterns don't disappear, they are re-routed.[58] That means the "unlearned" responses need to be continuously reinforced along with the new pathways.

Real learning requires a powerful process. It's not enough to read an article or attend a workshop – even a great workshop! The challenge is transference. The current research says about 30% of what's learned gets implemented,[59] and even then, only a very small percentage can be transferred from one application to another. Front desk staff may learn a new way of

Breaking down the process:

Phase: **Engage**

2 Steps:

- Increase Capability
- Experiment with Possibility

4 Milestones:

- Expand Competencies
- Prepare to Launch
- Jump In
- Strengthen Support

16 Actions suggested in the Operational Manual

greeting guests, but will hardly ever apply that to greeting their colleagues. Typical learning processes are rote, narrow, and over-focused on a one-off application. To be effective here we need learning systems that introduce new ways of seeing and new foundational skills (competencies), that we can support people to apply, practice, and integrate.

So this phase includes two key steps. The first is about the process of learning the new stuff and planning how to use it. The second step, perhaps even more rare, offers guidance of putting the new material in action and sustaining it over time. The steps and milestones in this phase are:

3. Increase Capability: Develop new awareness, skills, systems required to drive change.

- Expand Competencies: Learn new and strengthen needed skills.

- Prepare to Launch: Internalize new learnings and focus on where/how to apply them.

4. Experiment with Possibility: Test new methods, apply and innovate.

- Jump In: take action utilizing new skills, awareness, and systems.

- Strengthen Support: Reinforce new ways of operating.

As you know from the previous chapter, after walking you through these steps and milestones, we'll provide an "Operational Manual" with 16 specific actions that will support this phase.

Step 3: Increase Capability

This is a straightforward idea. Before the change you were using a particular level of awareness and skill, and particular systems, to get certain results. After the change you want new results – so you need new skills, new awareness, and perhaps new systems.

At the rational level, this capability might be more "systems" focused – a LEAN manufacturing process, a customer relationship management platform, a rapid prototyping design, a new structure for meetings, or a new diet. The rational, systems side is crucial… and inadequate.

Likewise, the emotional side is crucial, but also inadequate by itself. You could develop a team's social-emotional skills and they would get along better, which could be a great part of a change – but if you added to that some smart systems for team knowledge sharing and collaboration, you'd have a really powerful change. The problem, of course, is when people try to put in the system without the people-side, you get a lot of costs with very few benefits.

3.1 Expand Competencies

One of the big challenges in change is that the old way is well known. Let's take an example of changing diet to increase health; supposing you're someone who eats a lot of pasta and cheese and pizza. Probably you know what tastes good, and either you know where to get the ingredients and how to cook these foods, or you know some lovely restaurants, or maybe you spend a lot of dinners at your mother's house. So now, you decide to eat more vegetables and less starch. Great! But you're very busy today, and now it's 5:00 and you haven't gone shopping for dinner. You look in the fridge and there are a couple of parsnips. What can you possibly do with those? No time... better order a pizza.

On the other hand, suppose you're in the same situation, but beforehand you'd discovered two delicious, quick, low cost parsnip recipes you love. Easy! You stick with your change. So having new knowledge opens up new potential. To continue on the food theme (it's almost dinner time), it's as if you have a set menu of options of how to solve every problem you face each day. For some problems, there's just one option on your menu, so that's what you use. For other problems, you have 10 options, and you can choose. Maybe you typically use one, but those 10 options offer liberty to change; literally you have choice.

Whether you're talking about changing culture to increase customer orientation, or changing to implement a new a data tracking system, or changing to be a better friend, there is a variety of "stuff" to learn. "Stuff" can generally be broken into KAS – knowledge, attitudes, and skills. Almost certainly some of the KAS will be on the technical side and some on the relational side.

When we talk about "competencies" we're looking at building blocks of KAS that can be used in a wide variety of applications. Competency in written communication can be used to send a persuasive text, to create a book, to draft a speech... the competency is "content agnostic" in that it can be applied in many different domains. As people-experts, we tend to focus on people-side competencies like emotional awareness, influence, listening, and optimism. Those are crucial, but we don't pretend those are sufficient – depending on the change you're making, you'll need an array of new competencies to expand your menu of options.

These four actions will help with Expanding Competencies; see the "Operational Manual" section for more detail on each:

1. **Measure key competencies** (assess skills on the people side and technical side, identify critical gaps)

2. **Find trustworthy teachers, guides, and role models** (identify people who can help you acquire what you need to learn)

3. **Invest time over time** (create a process of learning versus a 1-shot experience)

4. **Focus on capacity-building** (rather than "picking up techniques" to solve one problem, develop core strengths that can be used to solve many problems)

Generally these four actions are pursued in conjunction with the actions in 3.2; together these will take from one to three months in one "large" cycle of the Change MAP. Typically there will be some new learning or capacity building over a few days, followed by blended learning and support to implement the rest of the steps. We recommend planning each sub-component, such as a workshop or meeting or coaching session, using the same MAP.

3.2 Prepare to Launch

The second milestone is taking the new KAS and focusing on how you'll use them to approach your specific needs. For example, suppose your change is to increase customer connection in your bank; you know that customers who use three or more of your products are much more valuable, so you set out to increase existing customers' use of your products. In the Engage phase you studied the problem and found that while customers like your bank, they don't fully trust you, partly due to a lack of follow-through on customer requests. You make a plan to address these issues, and in 3.1 you help your line managers learn new skills for proactive problem solving. You put together a great program and they all learned five critical skills. Tomorrow, in step 4, you want the managers to use what they learned. So now you're going invest a little energy ensuring that they can "cross the bridge" from training to real life. You recognize that different managers already employ some of the five skills, but not others. So, one of the key steps here is for each one to consider the skills they can either use better or start using, and specifically how they can try this out tomorrow.

Here are four actions to reach this milestone:

1. **Start from an internal drive** (identify: what do you WANT to do?)

2. **Target real-world, focused opportunities** (find places where new skills and awareness can be immediately applied)

3. **Adapt concepts** (put the ideas into your own words and "tweak" new learning to fit your context – plan to meet the objectives in a way that will work for you)

4. **Plan for others' reaction** (consider how others might feel as you begin utilizing what you've learned; what do you want them to feel? If there's a mismatch, plan how to navigate those feelings)

The story of the bank is a bit over-simplified because it describes this as a discrete experience that happens one day and is done the next. In actuality, these actions will occur over and over, mixed in and supporting the actions from the previous milestone (3.1).

Step 4. Experiment with Possibility

Now that you've got new capacity, your menu is expanded, and you've focused on how to apply them, so now it's time to start using the tools. If you've succeeded in steps one and two, this will actually be pretty easy – and fun! It's exciting to play with new toys.

It's important to maintain a "lightness of spirit" in this phase. This is not a "do or die" mindset! It's an opportunity for learning and discovery. That's why we call it "experiment" (a test or investigation designed to increase understanding) of "possibility" (a future of higher potential).

To facilitate the transition from learning to application, we've built a tool called Goalkeeper. Just as a soccer/football goalkeeper anchors the defense, the online Goalkeeper anchors your implementation process (read about it on www.igoalkeeper.com). Whether you use this tool or not, the principles we used in designing Goalkeeper will help you:

- Make a clear plan with simple, short-term steps.

- Get feedback on the plan.

- Get partners who agree to support you.

- Make your commitment visible to you and your supporters.

- Actively solicit feedback, yours and theirs.

- Keep it transparent and visible.

4.1 Jump In

This milestone is about taking action to continue learning. Not taking action to be perfect, but taking action to discover. Life is a laboratory, and every day we have the opportunity to adventure new experiments. Hopefully, in the way we're writing about this, you can feel that the attitude is crucial – we're not making light of the seriousness of this work, we're advocating for a serious joy. There are few things in life quite as wonderful as learning something worthwhile and applying that to make a positive difference. It's also painful and scary - what an intriguing paradox!

✓ Because change is a time of discovery and growth, it's challenging, but for the same reason times of change offer great fulfillment and pleasure.

Here are four actions that will facilitate step 4.1:

1. **Acknowledge the challenge** (don't expect to be perfect right away, respect the difficulty of doing something new)

2. **Declare commitment** (tell those involved, "I am working on x")

3. **Stay open to feedback** (notice the subtle responses)

4. **Celebrate failures with optimism** (mistakes are evidence of learning – value that progress)

These steps will be woven through the processes of Step 2 and won't require much additional time. These are most effectively conducted by setting aside a few minutes at a time, a few times a week.

4.2 Strengthen Support

If change were easy, you wouldn't be reading this book. Change is tough! Especially at this point: You've planned, you've learned, you've started to apply... and the change isn't working (yet). Change is a process, and even if you've "done everything right," it still takes time. That delay is tough. It's so hard to continue the new ways when you're not getting the reinforcement of success. That's one reason to follow the spiraling cycle. But even then, even with a small start, there will be a delay between risking new action and seeing the desired results.

So support at this point is crucial. In the Engage phase, one of your steps was to identify supporters. Now you really need one another! Support can be 1:1 with a friend, coach, colleague, or family member; it can be from groups; it can also be from tools and systems (hopefully this book is supporting you too!).

In addition to the need for support to maintain momentum, there's a dimension of change that is shared among people. Because we're social creatures, we exist in a web of relationships. Change, even individual change, requires a change to the whole web. When we talk about a team or organizational change, we're changing many webs. So there is a social dimension to all change.

As you work toward the "Strengthen Support" milestone, we recommend these actions:

1. **Include allies** (stay in touch with your coach, friend, partners; request feedback, maintain focus)

2. **Track micrometrics** (how often do you X each day?)

3. **Keep it on your agenda** (schedule time for this work)

4. **Acknowledge changing emotions** (notice that your and others' feelings may go "up and down," you're likely to experience a wide range of feelings in any change – notice them without over-correcting)

As with the 4.1 actions, these each require a few minutes "here and there" rather than a block of time.

Operational Manual

In this section you will find 16 actions to facilitate the Activate phase.

Step 3: Increase Capability | Milestone 1: Expand Competencies

3.1.1 Measure key competencies

If you want to expand capability, it's invaluable to discover the key competencies you need and to identify the critical gaps between the current reality and the need. Measuring what is important boosts accountability. Plus, these metrics keep the important resources "top of mind." Maintaining focus on what is important increases motivation and sense of direction.

Also consider that personal change starts from awareness, and awareness is not well supported by typical business practices. It's incredible how poor feedback is in most corporations. Ask people in your company: what is your strength? Lots of adults would be in a real difficulty to accurately answer such an easy question! More open, continuous feedback would add clarity.

So, before starting any change it is important to know:

1. What are the critical competencies to reach the goal?

2. How strong are these competencies in the company/team/person?

3. Are people aware of their strengths and weaknesses?

4. Is it clear why we are measuring these competencies?

✓ To do something new requires new skills and awareness. Measuring the skills and awareness is key to seeing what's needed!

3.1.2 Find trustworthy teachers, guides and role models

Learning is not a simple transfer of knowledge. It's a discovery. It's a risk. It's emulation. Every one of us that starts a new learning is asking: Will I be capable? Will it be difficult? Is the teacher trustworthy? Is it good for me? Will s/he help **me** or is this just focused on someone else's benefit (the company's, the trainer's, my boss's, etc.)?

It's natural to have some doubts. Learning requires going out of your comfort zone and finding a new equilibrium. Powerful learning is not the easy path. So having the right guide is critical in this kind of journey.

In our interview, Alan Deutschman shared a challenge of being stuck and then finding a way to change.[60] "I struggled for a decade, from my 20s to 30s, with being very overweight. I'm not quite 5'9" and at my peak I weighed 228 pounds, so I was technically an obese person. I really had this bad health problem and I knew that I had to do something about it. I struggled and failed for a decade.

"When I lived in New York I was writing a column for GQ magazine and they paid for me to work with one of the most expensive, prestigious personal trainers in New York at the Equinox chain of gyms, which was the very hot chain of gyms at the time. I was supposed to work out everyday with the top trainer and I wound up gaining weight from the experience.

"When I moved to San Francisco I accidentally found a trainer who I formed a strong relationship with. She communicated a strong conviction that I could change and I would change. This emotional link to her gave me hope and she was able to help me learn a whole different way of approaching my lifestyle. So it was a matter of really finding the right person who could help me learn. I wound up losing 40 pounds from the experience and keeping it off."

Deutschman's personal experience frames change in a new way: Rather than seeking a solution, change is about learning. So it's crucial to answer these questions before beginning the next part of the change journey:

- Who do you trust to teach you?

- What about these trustworthy teachers/managers can you emulate?

- If you are a leader and you want people to change, are you an effective teacher?

- Who is the teacher/trainer who can support your organizational development?

The "most competent" or "most famous" teacher is not necessarily the best:

Trust is as important as competence in learning.

3.1.3 Invest time over time

How long is a change? A blink! Change is rapid, but not transition. Learning is a process of transition toward change. You cannot expect to change a behavior with a two-day class. You need to create a learning path with mental model, self-reflection, personal support, feedback, practicum. The blended learning approaches with training, coaching, distance learning, workbooks, questionnaires, outdoor session, etc. are giving better results. Why? Because people have the time to experiment and reflect about what happened and the different methodologies catch different learning styles. This means we need to revise the old proposal of "quick training course" and add opportunities for action learning.

Unfortunately, most clients who call us for training ask, "Can we do this in one day? That's all the time we have?" The answer is yes! You can do one small part in one day, but if ALL you do is one day, it's a waste of resources. In our consulting we work with clients to consider how these one-days string together to create something meaningful rather than a series of quickly forgotten, disconnected "idea of the quarter" sessions. Often we'll advocate that instead of a two-day training, let's do a day followed by coaching, or separate the two days with practice time in between.

It's also important to remember that you need to maintain the change. Once key competencies have been raised, they need reinforcement through follow up, learning communities, and opportunities to apply the new capacities.

One of the missing points in organizations is the link between a training and day-to-day work. The challenge is integrating the contents of the training in the living relationships between leaders, collaborators, team members, customers, etc.

If you're building capability you need to consider:

- How do people learn?

- Have I designed a learning path or a course?

- If the learning is important, am I giving time worthy of the goal?

- How can I integrate the training activities in the business as usual?

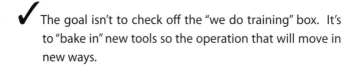 The goal isn't to check off the "we do training" box. It's to "bake in" new tools so the operation that will move in new ways.

3.1.4 Focus on capacity building

In this step you're implementing a learning process, but it can't be the typical corporate training.

Most training offers a "solution" comprised of fairly common sense actions prescribed as a magical answer; they're usually behavior-focused and fairly superficial. But it's not enough to give people the right answer: you need to give them the opportunity to find solutions. Sometimes it's really easy to say to a collaborator: "Do it my way!" But as we've learned from coaching, instead of the answer, if you give a good question the person will develop strength to reflect and decide. From a learning point of view this process offers FAR more value. It seems longer (and sometimes is longer) but the commitment will increase dramatically and probably the performance will be better and quicker.

Just for example, which investment will you choose?

A. $10,000 to teach 10 people a practical technique that solves one problem.

B. $20,000 to teach 10 people awareness and skills to solve a hundred problems on their own.

Frequently attractive training materials offer long "to do lists" with practical, common sense actions. Great! It looks like a lot of value. But consider: Why aren't your intelligent people already doing these things? Probably, because, as we discussed in the previous chapters, change creates emotional resistance. This resistance is an immunity system that protects us (or something in us). The issue isn't "a new technique" but insight and power to move out of the resistance. One key is to understand what we're getting from the old way, what we're protecting. The example of losing weight is brilliant. Every one of us knows that we need to move more and eat less. **The facts are simple. So why don't we all do it?** We're resisting, partly out of inertia, but partly because we get some benefits from not changing (and these are likely to be emotional benefits). What is that benefit we're seeking? Is there a better way to get that benefit that also gives us other important benefits?

In other words, giving someone a "how-to" or "the best way" or "the three secrets" is not that valuable because they probably already know it. Instead, give them a process to take their existing brilliance into action.

 Considering the frequency and speed of change in our companies, learning one system, one method, one technique is useless. We need to build learning capability this pace of change isn't slowing down or going away.

So consider your plans for this stage:

- Are we trying to transfer knowledge or enable people to learn?

- Are we coddling them to be lazy consumers of "learning bites" or teaching them how to learn?

- Are we pretending adoption is purely rational, or are we supporting people in understanding and managing the emotional dimension to apply new learning?

- Are we treading on the surface, or helping people in going beneath the water?

As the new learning is developed, the next step is to put it into action in real life.

Step 3: Increase Capability | Milestone 2: Prepare to Launch

3.2.1 Start from an internal drive

Based on the statistics, the odds of successful change are low, but with skill and effort it's possible. However: If you start from something you're not even interested in, even those slim odds vanish.

Try to understand what you WANT to do. If we want to pass from awareness to action we need to find a goal that motivates us deeply. When you're planning change with others, be sure you're inviting them to do the same – what do they care about? What excites them?

The expectancy theory[61] is a framework for considering your seriousness about a change:

> Is it important (for me)? (Vision)

> Is there a way someone could do this? (Blueprint)

> Can I do those things (will it work for me)? (Capacity)

If the answer to any is less that YES!, then more work is needed:

- For point one, the value, consider the long term – what is it you want in the future, where do you want to be a year, two, five from now? How will this change help with that?

- Point two is about the technical know-how, the blue-print. If you're not seeing a path, is there someone who can teach you? Has anyone ever done this?

- In point three you're considering your own capacity and the fit between you and the pathway. If you don't find that fit, consider: Can you break this down into smaller steps? Can you get support?

Or – maybe you're thinking about the wrong goal.

Often we pick "shoulds" to work on. "I'm weak at this, I should get better." Hmmm. Who said? Imagine going from "terrible at something" to "poor at it" - would that be really powerful? Sometimes.* But what about going from "strong" to "world

---

* This raises a research problem we often encounter: Imagine a scale of competence from 1-10. Going from a 1 to a 2 is a massive 100% change in percentage, and can look great on a report. But is that actually more valuable than a mere 12.5% change in going from 8 to 9? This dropping percentage of gain can mislead people think that boosting strengths isn't as significant.

class" – what effect might that create?

 Working with and through your strengths is a powerful
way to boost your motivation while increasing impact.

Often managers come out of training and, if they're lucky,
they've learned two or three important ideas and skills. Is there
ONE that excites you? Is there ONE that would actually be fun
to do? Shocking idea – if we start with those exciting, fun pursuits we might actually build up more energy!

3.2.2 Target real world, focused opportunity

Selecting a focused, actionable goal will increase the odds of
success. Probably you cannot change the world in two days, but
can you find one thing to improve? In others words, don't try
to emulate Steve Jobs tomorrow but identify one single goal
that will permit you to be a better leader tomorrow. Remember
we're working in a cyclical framework, and soon you'll be back
to the Activate phase expanding on this first success.

In time of complexity we need to maintain focus and avoid being overwhelmed by the millions of things to do. Otherwise
we risk saying: it's too complex at the moment, I will try next
year. Don't forget that knowledge without application tends to
disappear. Linking new knowledge with your real-world challenges is a way to link learning with results.

After you've gone through the effort of learning new skills and
awareness, consider:

 What is ONE place I can apply this tomorrow?

Try it now! What's one idea you've learned reading the book so far? What is one, specific, actionable place you can apply this idea tomorrow?

3.2.3 Adapt concepts to your own language and context

Sometimes after a training program you see unnatural behaviors by managers. They are trying to apply the lessons, but the result looks like a performance by a mediocre actor!

Imagine a workshop where the trainer provides a checklist telling the manager to focus on people. So the next day, the manager meets one of his collaborators and starts asking: "How are you doing? Your wife and your kids? The dog? OK? Great! So anyway: get the report on my desk in two hours…." Then the manager comes back to his office and looks at the People Management Checklist: "Take care of people." TICK - he's succeeded! Right? Or maybe not…

Rather than focusing on the behavior ("do this," "say this,") we need to focus on the goal. What is the result you want? What is the impact you want to have? Are you trying to create trust and connection, or to tick the box?

If the people around you don't feel trust and authenticity in what you are saying and doing, you are not getting the results you want. Yes, you need to understand the principle but at the same time you have your own leadership style, values, habits, and skills. So the challenge is blending the new approach with what's natural for you.

 Meet the new objectives in a way that will work for you.

Ask yourself:

- What is my goal?

- What are some different alternatives for achieving that?

- What is the most fitting solution?

- How do I do this in a way that's coherent with my style?

3.2.4 Plan for others' reaction

When you are preparing to launch a change, think about the possible reactions of others. Five years ago we had a great example of this issue. We were teaching how to improve people management capabilities and we said something about the importance of the questions. We received an e-mail a week later by a CFO who attended the class with only one phrase "I am sorry to say your technique is not working." Wow what a great way to start the day! We decided to call the CFO to better understand what happened; he was concerned about the way people were reacting to his questions. So we asked him to have an opportunity to meet his people – what we discovered was that the reactions were due to the fact that it was the first time in twenty years that the CFO asked something! Considering that they were going through a merger at the time, this "strange" new behavior made people worried.

Before acting, ask yourself:

- What might they feel? How will I feel about that?

- What do I want them to feel?

- What can I do to facilitate them to reach the desired

state?

- How can I monitor their real reactions to see if I've been effective?

✔ Emotions are real and powerful – so others' reactions are part of the result you're creating.

This can sound "Machiavellian," and we're not saying to fake it. Rather, to be both authentic and strategic, to be careful of this human dimension.

Now that you've effectively planned how to apply new learning, it's time to do it.

Step 4: Experiment with Possibility | Milestone 1: Jump In

4.1.1 Acknowledge the challenge

Every change is a challenge (otherwise we'd just call it "another day" instead of "change"). We know how our brain works. If you want to change a pattern you need to go out of your comfort zone. It's something that will create an emotional reaction. So, be prepared to fail, don't expect to be perfect. This is one of the reasons we advocate this spiraling, continuous process of change. As you go through the cycle over and over, you'll train yourself at changing.

We all experienced this as children – when we learned to walk we fell down. When we learned to ride a bike we skinned our knees. Respect the difficulty of doing something new. Respect your effort and the others' efforts. You cannot ask for perfection. It's an adaptive process that, at the beginning, is normally anything but perfect. If you want to change, do it anyway!

Some questions for you:

- How long have I been "doing it the old way?"

- How difficult will it be to change?

- What might it look like to make a small, but perhaps awkward, step?

- What is an acceptable result for the first week?

- How will I improve my first result?

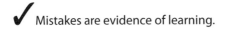 Mistakes are evidence of learning.

4.1.2 Declare commitment

When you have decided to launch a change, declare it: "I am going to work on..."

Why? At an emotional level, both you and others will have a tendency, even a driving pressure, to maintain the status quo. Not only do you get certain benefits of the "old way," others do too. So there could be very strong pressure from others to maintain the situation as is. In other words, even if it's a personal change that you're making by yourself, your change will change a whole web of relationships. The declaration puts others "on notice" that change is underway, which can help them notice it, accept it, and even support it.

At a simple level, we were coaching an executive through his SEI 360 results; he knew he wasn't really great with people, but he didn't realize how seriously he'd undermined trust until he saw the results, which were brutal – his team wanted him out. He decided to change. With our support, he went to his team members one by one, thanked them for the feedback, acknowledged his failure, told them the three specific steps he planned to take, and asked for a second chance. This was very humbling (and wouldn't be the solution in all situations). By declaring the change, not only did they give him another chance, several of them became real supporters of his effort.

A public declaration also commits you by creating a barrier to going back. A wonderful example comes from Sam Palmisano, CEO of IBM, when he decided to sell the PC Division to the Chinese company, Lenovo (giving them the opportunity to use the IBM brand). He was aware of the potential resistance from his shareholders ("but we are giving assets to a Chinese competitor!") and his managers ("but we are IBM, Big Blue, we can beat the Chinese competition!") He formalized the decision and put a huge advertising budget into a new "Business on demand" campaign to promote the strategic turnaround from manufacturing to business services. In essence, he staked his reputation on it: "If you want to come back to the old IBM, I will not be credible as CEO: if you want me as a CEO let's go in the value added services business."

Questions for thought:

- Who will be affected by your change?
- What specific commitments can you declare?
- Can you share a timeline and/or specific action steps?
- How can you update people about your goal?

✔ Declaring a goal increases the power for you, and creates an opportunity to bring others along.

4.1.3 Stay open to feedback

When you jump in a change, you'll immediately begin to get feedback that can help you assess the effectiveness of your experimentation and make minor course corrections along the way. Sometimes it's subtle.

It's not enough saying to people: "Is it ok? Tell me your opinion." It's too hard for them to answer clearly and honestly, so they'll likely soften their answer or remain silent. Sometimes people disagree but prefer to avoid the conflict. So your role as a leader is to pay attention to reactions, noticing the subtle responses too. Fortunately we know from Paul Ekman's studies that in the first second after an event people will express their emotional reactions moving the muscles of the face. Interestingly, this primal reaction is the same all over the world for the basic emotions.[62] That means that if you pay attention to faces you will get the feedback you want. So if you want to communicate something important, avoid e-mail and stay in touch with people in order to have the possibility to check their reactions.

If you do ask for feedback, consider ways to enhance the quality:

- Make sure that there's enough time for reflection before answering, and enough time for a real answer.

- Consider a tool, such as a 360.

- Consider a process, such as writing a note.

Some questions for you:

- Have you asked people for feedback?

- Have you considered the mood in the room after your announcement?

- Have you noticed the subtle reactions?

- Have you used these data to adjust your implementation?

✓ Don't wait for feedback, get it. It's there for you to access.

4.1.4 Celebrate failure with optimism

Optimism is a key competency in this process, so practice it at every setback. The optimistic view of failure is defined by three parameters[63]:

- Temporary: Yes, we failed, but it won't last forever. At SOME point this will get better.

- Isolated: The failure in this domain was serious, and there are other parts that are not failures. This failure doesn't taint or destroy everything.

- Effort: We worked, we failed – but we haven't tried everything yet. With additional effort it will be possible to improve this.

The challenge is to confront the failure without blame and rancor, but as a valuable part of the process – and move forward. In the book *Good to Great*, Jim Collins shares the wisdom of Admiral Jim Stockdale, the senior US prisoner of war in the Vietnam conflict. Stockdale said:

> You must never confuse faith that you will prevail in
> the end – which you can never afford to lose – with the
> discipline to confront the most brutal facts of your cur-
> rent reality, whatever they may be. [64]

✓ Optimism doesn't mean denying failure and struggle. It
means maintaining clarity of forward vision in the midst
of challenge.

The result of practicing optimism is that the failure, which could
sap your energy and take you off course, turns into fuel for continued growth.

Now that you're taking action, the next step is to ensure you
have the support to continue.

Step 4: Experiment with Possibility | Milestone 2: Strengthen Support

4.2.1 Include allies

Change is not only an individual effort. The risk is to be so focused on your change you lose contact with the others' reactions, and/or lose the support that others can give you. It's
important to over-communicate in times of challenge and
change.

As mentioned earlier, this is a good place for Goalkeeper* or an-

---

* Goalkeeper is an online accountability tool created by our team:
www.igoalkeeper.com

other tool for maintaining focus. Goalkeeper also facilitates the next two milestones.

Some self-assessment questions for you:

- To what extent are you looking at the impact of the change on other people?

- How are you using feedback to stay in touch with the reality?

- How effectively are you actively gathering emotional and technical support from the outside?

✔ Change is a shared challenge.

4.2.2 Track micrometrics

The risk in every change is to lose focus amidst the clamor of competing commitments. So, establish new routines and create some micrometrics to check daily, weekly and monthly. Reaching a goal is, of course, something that creates energy. Having the opportunity to establish quick wins is a great strategy for individuals too. So tracking simple accomplishments can fuel that energy. It's an emotionally intelligent choice to build up those useful feelings to keep you flowing through the Change MAP cycle!

A micrometric is something you can track by yourself with no special technology. For example, we were working with a leadership team on trust, so every meeting we began by asking each person to anonymously write a score from 1-5 rating their current trust level on the team. At the break we'd tabulate those and share them back.

Another micrometric is completion rate – for example, if you've decided to listen more, each time you listen put a tick mark on a whiteboard by your desk. How many tick marks today? Can you have another tomorrow?

 Of course this just measures quantity, not quality, so don't be confused… the tick mark isn't the goal! But tracking it can give you "real time" data to monitor your progress.

Questions for thought:

- Have I divided the main goal into sub-goals?

- What metric will show me progress on the sub-goals?

- How often will I check it?

- What happens if the results are not consistent?

4.2.3 Keep it on your agenda

One of the most common errors in a change process is to think that change can happen on top of business as usual. It's true that we cannot stop the world because we are trying to change, but on the other side, change needs time and energy. If the change is really something important, you have to schedule time in the agenda for it. The typical answer is: "Oh, I have no more time to schedule, I am full." Consider that we have choice; it's a matter of priority!

 There is no more time available. But every day we choose how we use the minutes.

We remember an executive who worked with us in coaching on the work-life balance issue. We had him calendar his son's birthday, a three-day vacation, and other important family commitments in his work agenda with the same seriousness he scheduled normal business meetings. The first reaction was: "It's terrible to write in the agenda that I'm going to a restaurant with my wife!" After a while he understood it was an issue of priorities.

Some questions to address:

- Am I really interested in the change?

- Have I scheduled time for change consistent with my seriousness?

- Is there something I can do to improve my time management?

- Have I dedicated appropriate time and energy to the change in the last week?

✓ At first weekly, then monthly, review these questions and evaluate the way you're dedicating time to your change process. Adjust as needed!

4.2.4 Acknowledge changing emotions

As you go through the change process you will feel a variety of emotions. The more serious the change, the more intensely you'll experience the emotions. Even in a trivial change you'll feel something because emotions are signals about your experience in the environment. Experiment: Try brushing your teeth or showering in a way that's different from your norm – notice your feelings. Can you identify at least five different feelings in that brief change?

 Change is likely to elicit a wide range of feelings. They provide data about the human experience of the process. Changing feelings is a sign of change.

- What are you and others feeling?
- What feelings are becoming more or less intense?
- What feelings are new or different?
- What are those feelings telling you?
- How are those feelings affecting implementation of the change?

 Note that it's important to identify a range of feelings – probably some are obviously helpful and some are helpful in less obvious ways.

As we discussed about fear, it doesn't make sense to "obey" every feeling. Treat your emotions as respected advisors – they might be right, they might be wrong… but don't pretend they're invisible.

This action is simple, but unconventional. Notice your own feelings. Name them. Write them down in a logbook.

In a team or organizational change, notice others' feelings. Name them.

Simply naming challenging feelings actually reduces the intensity.[65] It seems that naming the feeling gives us a sense of self-mastery – we know what's happening, we begin to make sense of it – and the message of the feeling is delivered. When we don't notice feelings they tend to "come out sideways." But noticing and naming them makes it easier for us to move on. For more about this, see "The Wisdom of Feelings" chapter in *At the Heart of Leadership*.[66]

Acknowledging others' feelings also builds connection and trust. When you name someone's feelings accurately, they know you "get it." It doesn't mean you agree, it's simply an acknowledgement of what is.

Wrapping Up on the Activate Phase

In the first phase you prepared, and in this phase you absorbed and applied new learning – you've created change. It's incomplete, a work in process, but it's happening! The first time through the Change MAP this change is subtle, the 10th time through is probably transformational.

A quick recap

Here are the components of this phase "at a glance":

Phase	Activate			
Goal	Experience Success			
Transition	Fear to Courage			
Steps	3. Increase Capability		4. Experiment with Possibility	
Milestones	3.1 Expand Competencies	3.2 Prepare to Launch	4.1 Jump In	4.2 Strengthen Support
Actions	3.1.1 Measure key competencies 3.1.2 Find trustworthy teachers, guides, and role models 3.1.3 Invest time over time 3.1.4 Focus on capacity-building	3.2.1 Start from an internal drive 3.2.2 Target real-world, focused opportunities 3.2.3 Adapt concepts 3.2.4 Plan for others' reaction	4.2.1 Acknowledge the challenge 4.2.2 Declare commitment 4.2.3 Stay open to feedback 4.2.4 Celebrate failures with optimism	4.2.1 Include allies 4.2.2 Track micrometrics 4.2.3 Keep it on your agenda 4.2.4 Acknowledge changing emotions

Final Thoughts

There are many paradoxes in this phase:

- Struggle and joy.

- Lightness and seriousness.

- Experimentation and need to succeed.

- Moving quickly and taking time for the process.

A paradox isn't the same as a contradiction – one of the wonderful aspects of humans is our capacity to hold contrasting elements at one time. These contrasts create a tension that is a form of energy. Perhaps the greater the paradox, the more intense the highs and the lows, and the more energy you can tap for change?

Phase: **Reflect**

Goal: Lock-in Wins

Transition: Judgment to Curiosity

Chapter 6: Reflect

The Goal:

If there's any wrap-up at all, after a typical implementation process, teams will meet for a brief review before closing the books. They evaluate the success of the project, congratulate or blame one another, and declare the task done. Maybe they even write a report that sits on a shelf in some office. There's a lot of value left on the table.

One of the biggest obstacles in moving from "a change" to "good at change" – or "changeability" – is how to crystallize the essence of one experience and then broaden and generalize, spreading those "gems" into new domains. At a personal level, consider a change you've made (moving house, starting a new job, quitting smoking, going back to school, etc.): can you clearly see what you learned from that experience, and can you apply that learning to a new challenge you face?

Another big obstacle is when you work hard to make a change, but then get distracted and lose the hard-won ground. You implement a new protocol and people are beginning to adopt it, but then a new product has to get to market and everyone gets focused on that. When they've finished, they seem to have completely forgotten the new protocol. It's kind of like when kids learn how to multiply fractions at the end of the school year and over vacation the new skill evaporates in the summer sun.

So when we talk about "Lock-in Wins" the goal is to overcome these two obstacles.

The other key ingredient here is that the work of this phase becomes the seeds of the next time around the cycle. So as you move through the Reflect phase, it's not simply a "let's recap" and maybe write a nice summary memo, but rather we need to distill key learnings and immediately begin looking forward to the next steps.

Beneath the Water:

There are many reasons people don't do adequate reflection. Perhaps the biggest is our social conditioning to come rapidly to summative judgment: Good. Bad. Right. Wrong. Once we've reached that conclusion, there's no room for inquiry; the case is closed.

We do an experience in workshops where we ask participants to identify a "dramatically unusual" feature in a common object that we show, and we ask them to raise their hands once they've identified the feature. It's fascinating to watch participants in this experience: Over and over, people study the object, then raise their hands **and then step away**. Once they "have the answer" they stop looking! Here's the surprise: When we ask, almost none of them has seen the really significant discrepancy. They see a minor detail and decide "that's it, I'm done."

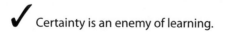 Certainty is an enemy of learning.

When you are going through change, sometimes you don't notice the progress you've made. This can have two negative effects: First, you don't gain the energy from the success. Second, you don't have time to assimilate along the way; you arrive at a new destination and it doesn't "feel right" so you slip back.

A colleague was telling us about the experience of losing 50 pounds. She said that one day, after losing about 30 pounds, she was sitting on an airplane and was surprised when she could reach down and pick up her bag from the floor. She spent the rest of the flight just noticing how it felt different, and getting used to herself in this stage. Her experience helped her lock in a "new normal." Continuing that process she found it easier, for the first time in her life, to keep the weight off. It's also worth noting that this change came after a powerful "Engage" phase where she examined a whole range of feelings and patterns in her life, and finally made a new commitment to purpose. The weight loss was a sidebar to a huge transformation of taking her place in the world.

Transition: Judgment to Curiosity

It's likely that judgment is a basic process of the human brain. Our brains are built to categorize and sort in order to create order and efficiency, and judging is part of that. There are also important benefits of judging – it's how we set limits. So it's unlikely that we can, and perhaps we shouldn't, eliminate judgment. That said, judgment is closed and fixed and it blocks learning.

Just think what happens to you when someone says, "I want to give you some feedback." Can you feel your muscles tense?

When we're facing a judge (your boss, your dad, or the person in a black robe in a courtroom), we know that s/he has power over us. That's a threat, and our brain responds by activating the "fight-flight-freeze" system to protect us. The executive areas of the prefrontal cortex shut down, neurohormones for protection begin flooding our bodies, and we get ready for battle. Our resources for creative and critical thinking have left the building. We've done all this work to move out of frustration and fear, and SLAM, we're back to that cycle.

Defining Terms

There are probably several forms of **judgment**, but in this case we're talking about the form tied to a summative, firm conclusion. Judgment means: "the cognitive process of reaching a decision or drawing conclusions."[67] In an ideal world, we do this carefully, weighing all the variables and coming to a valid, valuable conclusion.

In reality, most judgment is rendered quickly, based on severely limited information, and absolutely subjectively. We were working with a challenging CEO who frequently came to instant judgment about various employees. To make it worse, he pretended that he hadn't done so. He'd spout these harsh, subjective conclusions about how someone was dumb or incompetent, then notice himself, and say, "but I'm not judging, we have to see what he does…" Yet somehow his original declaration never changed – when those who were "good" failed, the CEO blamed someone who he'd decided was "bad."

So the risk of judgment isn't so much the process of judging, but the inflexible conclusion. Yes, we all judge, that's how our brains work. Some of us stick with our first judgment and ignore any evidence that doesn't reinforce our existing opinion. Not only does it have a toxic emotional effect, it's just ignorant.

In this context, we're talking about the **feeling of judgment**, which is that sense of superior or inferior certainty. It feels closed, hard, controlling (or being controlled), and superior (or inferior).

On the other hand, **curiosity** is a feeling of exploration and discovery. It does not call for judgment, but for deeper consideration. Curiosity is tied to anticipation (looking forward) and excitement. It includes identifying what does and doesn't fit.

As Isaac Asimov said:

> The most exciting phrase to hear in science, the one that heralds the most discoveries, is not "Eureka!" (I found it!) but "That's funny..."

There are specific brain regions tied to curiosity. The hippocampus, located in the emotional region of the brain, tells us what to pay attention to. It's highly influenced by emotion and by novelty. When we're curious, dopamine, a "feel good" chemical, is released, and pleasure/reward centers of the brain fire. In an intriguing study, researchers at the California Institute of Technology used fMRI to see the brain at work, and when people were curious their memory centers were also more active; they followed the imaging with a behavior study and confirmed that curiosity increased retention.[68]

 Curiosity causes us to focus on what's beyond the norm and unexpected.

Watch Out

A few key considerations:

- Curiosity is undermined by rushing to conclusions, cutting off discussion, and being pressured to find "the answer."

- Judgment is increased through blame. In fact, research shows that when people observe blame, they become more likely to blame; there is a "socially contagious" effect where blame leads to more blame.[69]

- Open-ended questions increase curiosity, especially "fusion" questions that integrate emotion and cognition.

- "Why" questions, and questions that ask for a conclusion, can increase judgment – they are useful, but not at the start of exploration.

- While respectful dialogue and exploring ideas are important parts of creative discovery, sometimes people confuse "discussion" with "debate." An intriguing set of recommendations comes from the highly successful IDEO design firm; one of their principles is to eliminate the "Devil's Advocate" role, that person who loves to point out what's wrong with the ideas, because they've found this faux-helpful stance reduces real innovation and pushes people into defensiveness.[70]

Consider

Karen McCown, the Founding Chairman of Six Seconds, likes to ask this question that summarizes the challenge of this transition: "Do you want to be right, or do you want to solve the problem?"

 Sometimes it "feels good" to judge and "be right." That seduction can pull you away from your cycle of growth.

Reflect | Steps and Milestones:

In this phase you're discovering what you've learned, bringing that to the surface, and then building on it. You're working to make sure all the stakeholders are aware of the progress, and adding the new experiences to the cultural and systemic "DNA."

If you are early in the spiral, this phase is largely about increasing focus and clarity of your plan. Later, after cycling through the process several times, this phase is about culture and systems change.

This phase is frequently cut short because it's seen as an unnecessary expense: "We've already got the results, we don't need to measure them." So it may be helpful to consider the Reflect phase isn't just the end of the cycle: It's the start of the next cycle, positioning you to BUILD on the successes.

Breaking down the process:

Phase: **Reflect**

2 Steps:

- Celebrate Progress
- Re-Imagine the Future

4 Milestones:

- Discover Results
- Share Lessons Learned
- Integrate Achievements
- Look Forward

16 Actions suggested in the Operational Manual

The components of this phase are:

5. Celebrate Progress: Clarify what's happened and bring that to the surface.

- Discover Results: Assess and explore what you've learned in the Activate phase.

- Share Lessons Learned: Ensure that all the stakeholders are aware of the progress.

6. Re-Imagine the Future: Update the future vision based on progress to date.

- Integrate Achievements: Make the lessons learned part of your standard operations and strategic plan.

- Look Forward: Build on the vision and determine if, and how, to move forward.

Step 5: Celebrate Progress

If you've gone through the first four steps, you've made progress. Maybe not exactly as you imagined it, but something's happened. What? What about that change is working? What can you build upon and expand?

In this step you are evaluating (without judging!), checking the metrics and progress against the plan from the Engage phase. One key is for the various stakeholders to step out of the day-to-day and really notice the change, to bring it top of mind. If you've been using a "pilot project" structure, then those in the pilot now get to share the experience.

As you review the past four steps, you are also crafting a story, a narrative, of the change (in a complex change there might be several stories). This story serves to capture key gems from the change so far. It also carries some of the new emotional energy gained. In Step 6, you'll refine that and share it with others as a way of building on the success.

Most importantly, we call this "Celebrate Progress" because we want you to have the emotional experience of a great festival or carnival. You have a chance here (especially if there have been significant improvements) to really boost the emotional energy and add fuel to the cycle.

5.1 Discover Results

What happened? Find out!

Remember there are many dimensions to explore – what the data says, what people have experienced, what people have noticed (or not), and how those involved feel about all this. For example, maybe the results are exciting for some but disappointing for others, this creates and opportunity create more clarity around what's expected in the next cycle.

The actions we suggest to "Discover Results" are:

1. **Make results vivid** (re-measure, show, discuss, synthesize)

2. **Discuss the emotional impact of results** (consider how people feel about what's changed (or not)

3. **Self-evaluate** (identify where are you satisfied and dissatisfied with your work in the change)

4. **Find the success in the failures** (what value can be extracted from what didn't work well?) and failures in success (what can we do better next time?)

Generally these four actions will take some background research and then a half-day meeting.

5.2 Share Lessons Learned

Working on this milestone you're crystallizing the learning, formalizing the discoveries from the first milestone. Then you begin to tell the story of the change. In 6.1 you'll really focus on rippling it outward. Here you're still focused on the past – since the Engage phase began, what can we celebrate?

Four actions for this milestone:

1. **Identify new benchmarks and best-practices** (mine the results to identify what should be carried forward)

2. **Prepare to communicate results** (consider both tactically and emotionally how to ensure everyone involved can get the benefit of the results)

3. **Acknowledge emotional costs of change** (even in "positive" change there is loss, grieve the loss and let go of the old)

4. **Revel in the successes** (celebrate; tell stories to communicate the change; acknowledge contributions; reinforce gratitude)

These actions can occur in two to three meetings with some individual follow-up actions.

Step 6. Re-Imagine the Future

In step 5 you were focused on what happened – now it's time to turn to what happens next. You've explored the learnings and pulled them together into a "story" (maybe your story has words, pictures, charts, plans… but it's a narrative that people will "get" both emotionally and intellectually). Now it's time to plant that into your systems.

If you're working at an organizational level, this work is about organizational culture and systems. On the cultural side: What stories from this cycle do you want passed around at the water cooler? On the systems side: How do you need to update your calendaring or manufacturing line or A/P or whatever methods? These decisions might spin off new cycles of work and change to implement.

If you're working on an individual change, instead of "culture" you're probably focused on relationships. Remember that the web of relationships needs to change for the individual change to be sustained – who needs to know about the progress? A small example: If you've made a change commitment to lose weight and have successfully transformed your menu, maybe your friends need to know that at this point in your life you'd rather have a great fruit basket instead of candy for your birthday? The systems here are actually similar to the organizational level – your calendar, your budget, your daily schedule…

The final push is to go further into the future. You've made some change, you're standing on new ground (maybe higher ground?) From this perspective, you feel a bit different and you can see a little differently. Leverage this new position to gain even more forward vision and to make sure you've updated your plans.

Remember, Reflect is the "Aim" phase – not the end, but a key step in keeping the cycle moving in a worthwhile direction.

6.1 Integrate Achievements

This Milestone takes clear strategic thinking. You take the clear picture from Step 5, the gems of learning, and connect them to your daily operation. Note that this Milestone begins with something "strange" – a focus on emotions. That's because we want to be sure the "IQ work" is solidly grounded and re-inforced by the "EQ work." Emotion changes the way you see, what you remember, how you learn, how you communicate... take strategic advantage of the emotional gains you've made in the cycle so far to be sure that your process of integration stays human-friendly.

These are the four actions to "Integrate Achievements":

1. **Strengthen useful feelings** (notice and heighten the feelings that will fuel the next phase of change)

2. **Integrate into systems and culture** (make the successes part of daily life at a tactical level and introduce new stories to shape the culture with examples of successes)

3. **Strengthen and build on lessons learned** (plan how to replicate and scale)

4. **Revisit strategic plan** (update considering how the results of this cycle affect the ongoing strategy)

Generally these actions occur over several meetings taking up less than a week, but some will require a whole new cycle of change (e.g., integrating into systems and culture).

6.2 Look Forward

Finally, it's time to stretch. Where could this all go? How has our vision expanded? Pursuing this milestone you're opening up creativity and innovation – and finally deciding what to do next, which will, of course, start you on the next "spin" of the cycle.

We suggest these actions to complete this phase:

1. **What if...** (time to dream: if you could change something, what would it be? No boundaries, no limits. What could happen if the changes were fully scaled?)

2. **Create a future timeline** (work backward from above - where do we want to be in 10 years, 5 years, 2 years, 1 year?)

3. **Reconnect to purpose** (revisit alignment of personal and organizational purpose, what has this change meant for you and your purpose, us and our purpose?)

4. **Stop, start, continue?** (Decide: Will we continue? If so, what's next?)

Typically these four actions comprise the agenda of the final team meeting, and can be combined with the start of the next cycle.

Operational Manual

In this section you will find 16 actions to facilitate the activate phase.

Step 5: Celebrate Progress | Milestone 1: Discover Results

5.1.1 Make results vivid

To have a strong focus on accountability we need to measure what happened in the change. If we used metrics at the beginning, it's important to re-measure to see what's concretely changed. The tools we discussed (Section II, Chapter 1) offer the opportunity to see the situation before the change and after a while.

It's a great way to calculate the Return On Investment (ROI) of the project. This is a best practice for every change process at people level or at the company level. Sometimes the tendency is to think that all the people are aligned and on the same page. But every time we've done this, people have found great satisfaction in having the opportunity to better understand the situation. People love to see figures and graphics of what happened. Remember: you have to use numbers that people can understand. Giving the opportunity to discuss the results is always useful as it permits people to internalize the information.

So, before planning a follow-up activity it's important to ask yourself:

- What are the metrics I want to re-measure?

- Are these metrics meaningful to employees?

- How can I engage people in the discussion?

- What are the three most important messages I want to leave?

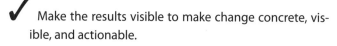 Make the results visible to make change concrete, visible, and actionable.

5.1.2 Discuss the emotional impact of results

The discussion of the emotional impact of the results is usually surprising (especially if you tend to focus on the rational brain). You might expect joy with positive results or sadness/anger with failure. But we know that the emotional response is linked to expectations, so here's a formula:

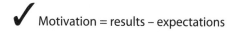 Motivation = results − expectations

So if you reach a result of "7" but people were expecting "9," probably you will have disappointment in the room… and vice-versa. This is the reason why satisfaction with the first win tends to diminish by the second: after the first success we come to expect that! The challenge is to maintain both high standards and high motivation.

Also consider that every person could have a different reaction. The risk is an unpleasant emotional contagion if one of your leaders had huge expectations. We need to have time to manage these emotional chains.

Let's consider these questions:

- What reactions are you expecting?

- What is the emotional cost of the change?

- How can you manage the emotional chain reactions?

- How do you want them to feel at the end of the pre-sentation?

Ask! How do you feel about the results?

Then discuss why different people have different feelings.

5.1.3 Self-evaluate

It's time to ask: were you are satisfied or dissatisfied with your work in the change? It's an important reflection for a leader and a powerful tool.

When you recognize and authentically share your own experience, it's likely to have a significant impact on people. Acknowledging your own successes and failures creates an immediate emotional bonding, and is an important step in your own learning.

Make a list of areas where you are satisfied and dissatisfied with your work as a change leader.

- What is the best thing you did?

- What is one place you fell short, or a major error you made? What will you do differently next time?

- How can you share these reflections with your collaborators and stakeholders?

 Self-awareness is the key for a change leader.

5.1.4 Find the success in the failures
. . . .

Don't be scared by failure. Only those who try can fail. Consider that in every failure there are valuable lessons: lessons about ourselves, about the reactions of other people, about the real value of a goal. If you are committed to use these lessons, you will be a better change agent tomorrow.

The case of 3M is great. They worked, and failed, to create a new strong glue. The accidental result: a piece of paper with a weak glue. Trash? No! Post It! An innovation used worldwide. What an amazing failure. So if we want to have a return on investment on our failure, we need to ask ourselves:

- What I can learn from the failure?

- How can I use this lesson learned?

- How can I avoid the same error next time?

- Is there something valuable in this failure?

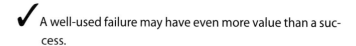 A well-used failure may have even more value than a success.

Step 5: Celebrate Progress | Milestone 2: Share Lessons Learned

5.2.1 Identify new benchmarks and best-practices

The purpose of this action is to review and solidify the lessons from 5.1. For every key lesson, consider:

- What would this look like in operation?

- What are the best practices that would support this?

- What is our expectation for performance in this area in the next 90 days? (Set the new benchmark.)

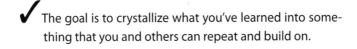 The goal is to crystallize what you've learned into something that you and others can repeat and build on.

5.2.2 Prepare to communicate results

How can other stakeholders best come to understand what you've learned? One risk is to come out sounding superior: "We're so great, you should all be like us." On the other extreme, the risk is to keep your learning secret and leave others in the dark.

- Who will benefit from knowing? (And, whose knowing will benefit the ongoing change?)

- How do you want others to feel about the results of

this cycle?

- What are the most important things for them to know?

- What mechanisms are available to you to communicate?

- What messages will you pass through those channels, to those stakeholders, to achieve those results?

In practical terms, you will probably need to make a chart of the above for each key lesson, and use that chart in the next actions and steps. Then, craft some "stories," narratives that capture the essence in a way that will be effective for your various audiences.

5.2.3 Acknowledge emotional costs of change

Take time to reflect on the losses. If you've successfully made some change, then you have let go of something. Maybe it was great, maybe terrible, but it was part of you (or your team, or your organization). Acknowledge that you've let go of that "old stuff." Sometimes that is happy, but sometimes sad; if needed, grieve the loss. It's another intriguing emotional paradox, even when we prefer the new reality, we're going to miss certain aspects of the old (often idealized) way.

✔ If you don't acknowledge the loss, you don't make an emotional separation from the old way and it is easier to slip back into it.

This can be as simple as a brief conversation, or a moment of reflection, or writing down these things we've moved from, and throwing them in the fire. It really depends on the intensity of your change; this can be something really "light" or intensely emotional, it's an important part of feeling closure about the past.

5.2.4 Revel in the successes

Now it's time to celebrate! Maybe this is a meeting where you share the successes and deliver the communication you planned in 5.2.2. You could also do the 5.2.3 action early in this event, and then really focus on the achievements. A passing "congratulations" is not enough. It can be difficult to take time to celebrate when you feel the pressure to urgently pursue next steps. And it has real value.

 Take this seriously! It's an important opportunity to boost the emotional energy and create fuel for your next iteration of the cycle.

We planned this kind of event with one of our clients, and the CEO stood up and congratulated the team, but then closed by fiercely stating "we can't rest now, the progress you made isn't enough." People took it okay because they knew he genuinely appreciated them, but it was a dangerous moment. This can undermine the message of appreciation and recognition; like when you're grandmother says, "you're so successful, *but* why don't you…."

In planning your celebration process, remember to:

- Acknowledge achievement and effort.

- Continue to raise the bar without putting down the progress.

- Fuel the feelings of gratitude, hope, and excitement.

Step 6: Re-Imagine the Future | Milestone 1: Integrate Achievements

6.1.1 Strengthen useful feelings

This might not be one specific action, but something you do repeatedly in step 6. As we wrote in 5.2.4, if you've succeeded in this process, there will be some emotional shifts (maybe slight, maybe dramatic); just as you need to "lock in" the lessons learned, you want to lock in this emotional progress. Consider the "dotted arrows" going from the Cycle of Resistance out to the Cycle of Engagement. If the start of the arrow is a "1" and the tip is a "5," how far have you come in the emotional journey? What are some new, useful feelings that are surfacing or strengthening (in you, the team, the organization)?

Go back to the EVS (Engagement Vital Signs) chart on page 102; which feelings are different now?

✓ Acknowledging, naming, and accepting those useful feelings will strengthen them.

You might do this several times "in small ways" through the rest of this step, just a moment of recognition has material benefit.

6.1.2 Integrate into systems and culture

Depending on where you are in the spiral of change, this may be the most complex step in the Reflect phase. You're goal is to find ways to take what you've learned, the success of the cycle so far, and implant that into your systems, structures, and culture.

It's very likely that this discussion will "spin off" some new projects that can be planned using the MAP.

Here are some examples of some common systems into which you can plant the new learnings:

- Calendar

- Budget

- Daily schedule

- Weekly scheduled events (e.g., stand up meetings)

- Reward/recognition

- Supervision

- Ongoing learning (coaching, mentoring, on-the-job feedback)

- Policies and procedures

In your context there are likely to be other organization-specific systems such as Q/A, controls, customer feedback loops, etc.

One critical system in organizations is the water cooler. In the Engage phase, you listened to hear the stories that are prevalent, and considered the emotional message of those stories. It may be time for some new stories. Stories shape culture, they tell people, "this is how things are done here," and climate, "and here's how people feel about that." Are there some new stories that came about in the Activate phase that can be authentically and organically shared to add a new "vector" to the organizational culture?

6.1.3 Strengthen and build on lessons learned

Where the previous action was more about systemic growth, this action is intended to focus on the individuals who have been involved in the change. Depending on the type of change you're leading, you might do either 6.1.2 or 6.1.3 or both.

For each lesson learned, what's the next step for you? How do you "take it higher" and build on that lesson?

What will happen when you do so?

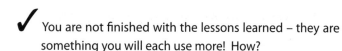 You are not finished with the lessons learned – they are something you will each use more! How?

6.1.4 Revisit the strategic plan

Presumably you have some kind of plan guiding you, your team, and/or organization. If not, perhaps it's time! Most likely you have several – your strategic visions, team and individual operational agendas or annual goals, and maybe 90-day priorities.

Now that you've moved through the cycle of change, revisit those plans. Check:

- Is this change cycle moving us forward?

- Are we moving in a new direction? Is this the direction

we want to go?

- How do the results of this cycle of change inform our plans?

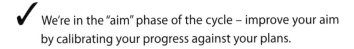 We're in the "aim" phase of the cycle – improve your aim by calibrating your progress against your plans.

Again, depending on where you are in the spiral, this could be a 30-minute conversation or a 2-day retreat that encompasses all the actions of step 6.

Step 6: Re-Imagine the Future | Milestone 2: Look Forward

These four actions are likely taken together in one meeting.

6.2.1 What if...

This is an opportunity to be creative and visionary with no constraints. Given what you've learned and achieved so far, where would you like to go? If the change was successful beyond your dreams, what would you do?

 The purpose of this action is to expand the vision.

This can be done in a variety of ways, such as individually drawing a symbol and sharing, or just going around the table and offering one potential.

6.2.2 Create a future timeline

Now we want to you to take that expanded future vision and make it more concrete. What of that vision could, if all goes well, happen in 10 years?

In 5 years?

2 years?

Next year?

What are key next accomplishments for us to focus on?

6.2.3 Reconnect to purpose

Reflect: What has the progress in the cycle meant to you and your purpose, us and our purpose?

If you were successful in those next steps (from 6.2.2), how would that serve your purpose – individually, as a team, and as an organization?

 Is it important to continue on this change path?

6.2.4 Stop, start, continue?

Having considered where this could go, what might next steps look like, and why? It's time to decide. Will you/we continue this change process?

If so, what's next?

What is your level of commitment?

This discussion leads directly into the start of the next Engage phase where you are working first to Enroll People. In this discussion, we suggest you consider the three key points from Step 1, Milestone 1, Action 1; here they are again:

- Engagement is based on deep motivators. As you consider the current change, how engaged are the people involved? How does this change connect with deep motivators? How can you add meaning and depth to connect to these core drivers?

- You cannot force people to change. You can inspire them, you can create meaning but you cannot change people. Choice is the key to move people. Can you transform The Change into **Our** Change? Remember that certain emotions are signals to protect/defend/attack and cause a narrowing of focus, while others create forward momentum toward opportunity – for example excitement, hope, trust, curiosity, joy, caring, and wonder are all "expansive" feelings. How can you fuel and tap those?

- Emotions are not logical. You work with emotions at an emotional level, not through being right and having the rational plan. Even when the emotion is based on "wrong facts" the emotion is real.

A quick recap

Here are the components of this phase "at a glance":

Phase	Reflect			
Goal	Lock-in Wins			
Transi-tion	Judgment to Curiosity			
Steps	5. Celebrate Progress		6. Re-Imagine the Future	
Mile-stones	5.1 Discover Results	5.2 Share Lessons Learned	6.1 Integrate Achievements	6.2 Look Forward
Actions	5.1.1 Make results vivid 5.1.2 Discuss the emotional impact of results 5.1.3 Self-evaluate 5.1.4 Find the success in the failures	5.2.1 Identify new benchmarks & best-practices 5.2.2 Prepare to communicate results 5.2.3 Acknowledge emotional costs of change 5.2.4 Revel in the successes	6.1.1 Strengthen useful feelings 6.1.2 Integrate into systems & culture 6.1.3 Strengthen and build on lessons learned 6.1.4 Revisit the strategic plan	6.2.1 What if… 6.2.2 Create a future timeline 6.2.3 Reconnect to purpose 6.2.4 Stop, start, continue?

Wrapping Up on the Reflect Phase

You've now clarified the results, build upon them, and decided if you'll continue. The next step, of course, is to go back to the start of the cycle and "take it up a notch." Next time through you'll have more forward momentum because you've transitioned toward the Cycle of Engagement. This will allow you to be more detailed and sophisticated in the next phase.

Final Thoughts

We call this phase "Reflect" because it's an opportunity to take time out from the action, to step "up" out of the daily business and look back at what's happened, then look forward to where you're going.

This phase may well be the most under-utilized opportunity in contemporary organizational life. We tend to operate in a furious blur of action taking little opportunity to acknowledge the journey, to check direction, and to refocus. But aiming is not a "nice to have," this is absolutely critical for success of any endeavor.

Part III

YOU

In the previous chapters we have seen how to manage the people side of business in changing organizations. Now, in this last section we are going to focus on the most important person in achieving the results of change: YOU. You as a leader, you as a change leader, you as the person going through the change you lead. We invite you to reflect on three crucial points:

1. How are you using your emotions to accelerate change?

2. How are you using the power you have as a leader?

3. Where are you taking people through the changes you are leading?

The success of the change is intimately connected to your performance as a leader. We tried to provide a detailed roadmap to manage the different phases of the process and the transformation of the emotions of the people around you. Now it's time to think how to be the change you wish to see. In the next chapters we will provide you with some tools and provocative thoughts to be a real leader worth following.

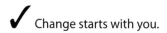 Change starts with you.

Listening to the inner voice
– trusting the inner voice –
is one of the most important
lessons of leadership.

- Warren Bennis

Chapter 7:
Tools for Emotions

Imagine you're a team member walking into a meeting to discuss an upcoming change, and you're frustrated by the lack of progress, disappointed by the contention on the team, worried about the current results – and paradoxically excited about the potential. Now, imagine the change leader walks in and he is stressed, rushed, and worried. How will that affect you and the other team members?

At best, "not helpful."

What feelings *would* be helpful from the Change Leader?

Where do those feelings come from?

We'd like to offer a few key points about emotional intelligence, and offer some tools for being more effective with emotions. To learn more about emotions and emotional intelligence, there is an extensive library of free articles as well as books and other tools on the Six Seconds website: www.6seconds.org

Concepts

One of the basic concepts for the emotionally intelligent change leader is a deeper understanding of emotions; we call this Emotional Literacy. Another is a framework for applying emotional intelligence; we'll share the Six Seconds EQ Model in brief.

Emotional Literacy

There are many different ways of categorizing emotions. Some researchers say there is one basic emotion (fear), others say four (glad, mad, sad, afraid), but a common framework is eight core emotions with thousands of combinations and variations.

The eight basic emotions tend to be quite consistent between people; there are basic muscular and biochemical responses that all humans experience corresponding to at least six of these.

Each basic emotion serves a survival function; they signal us to pay attention and motivate us or prepare us to deal with a particular issue. Here is a synopsis:

Basic Emotion	Basic Message
Anger	What is in the way?
Anticipation	What important thing is coming?
Joy	What do you want to maintain?
Trust	What do you want to embrace?
Fear	What is at risk?
Surprise	What is unexpected?
Sadness	What (that you love) are you losing?
Disgust	What rules are broken?

✔ Note that all of these basic messages have some survival value. When you're unsure of the reason for a feeling, ask: How is this helping the person survive?

When you have an experience (e.g., you get an email from your boss: "come see me now") there is about ½ a second where you interpret this stimulus, then you have an automatic emotional response. The emotion serves to focus and energize you to prepare to deal with the situation. Then you think about the stimulus, and your thinking is shaped and colored by the emotion. This gives rise to an array of new feelings.

When you get started with emotional literacy, the eight basic emotions are a useful guide. When you notice feelings, if you can pin down a few of the basic emotions that are in the mix, you can at least see which categories of emotion are at work. "I feel some of this and some of this." Then you can consider the table above.

You will (almost) always have multiple emotions and recombining feelings, so sorting them out can be quite troublesome. There are thousands of these combinations and they also vary in intensity, so it's highly dynamic. For consideration, here are a few combinations:

Feeling	Possible Recipe
Impatience	Anger (way is blocked) + Anticipation (looking ahead)
Worry	Fear (risk) + Anticipation (looking ahead)
Boredom	Disgust (rejection) + Sadness (loss) + Fear (risk)
Hope	Anticipation (looking ahead) + Joy (wants fulfilled)
Respect	Trust (accepting) + Joy (wants fulfilled) + Anticipation (looking ahead)

We say "possible recipe" because feelings are subjective, these are likely accurate, but what you call "Impatience" might be a little different from what we call it.

EQ Competencies

 Emotional intelligence is the capacity to be smart with feelings – to blend emotions and thinking to make optimal decisions.

It's a foundational intelligence that drives personal and professional performance.[71] As an *intelligence*, EQ isn't a set of "techniques," but rather a way of seeing and solving problems. Just as mathematical intelligence lets you accurately interpret numbers and solve math problems, emotional intelligence lets you accurately interpret feelings and solve people-puzzles.

To help people put the concept of emotional intelligence into action, Six Seconds developed a practical model; a process framework for making emotionally intelligent decisions. It begins with three "pursuits" – each is an action step to use emotional intelligence effectively:

Know Yourself

Clearly seeing what you feel and do. Emotions are data, and these competencies allow you to accurately collect that information.

Choose Yourself

Doing what you mean to do.

Instead of reacting "on autopilot," these competencies allow you to proactively respond.

Give Yourself
· ·

Doing it for a reason.

These competencies help you put your vision and mission into action so you lead on purpose and with full integrity.

Within the three pursuits are eight specific, measurable, learnable competencies. These are explained in detail in *At the Heart of Leadership*[72], and measured through the SEI (Six Seconds Emotional Intelligence Assessment).[73]

Pursuit	Competency	Definition
Know Yourself	Enhance Emotional Literacy	Accurately identifying and interpreting both simple and compound feelings.
	Recognize Patterns	Acknowledging frequently recurring reactions and behaviors.
Choose Yourself	Apply Consequential Thinking	Evaluating the costs and benefits of your choices.
	Navigate Emotions	Assessing, harnessing, and transforming emotions as a strategic resource.
	Engage Intrinsic Motivation	Gaining energy from personal values & commitments vs. being driven by external forces.
	Exercise Optimism	Taking a proactive perspective of hope and possibility.
Give Yourself	Increase Empathy	Recognizing and appropriately responding to others' emotions.
	Pursue Noble Goals	Connecting your daily choices with your overarching sense of purpose.

While a detailed explanation is beyond the scope of this book, we bring it up as one of the most important frameworks for change leaders. As we've discussed, change begins from the inside – and emotional intelligence allows you to see and manage the feeling-side of this process.

A free tool for exploring emotional literacy is online at www.6seconds.org/feel – the "Emotoscope" lets you identify emotions and then provides insight into their meaning and value. There is a Facebook version that lets you track your feelings over time.

Tools

This book would be very long if we went into detail about every tool we teach for the emotional side of the change journey. We've provided many examples and strategies in the actions laid out In Part Two. But we wanted to offer a few more tools that can be applied more generally.

All of these tools can be used at almost any stage of the change journey. You can use these tools yourself to understand and Navigate your feelings, and you can use them with others to help them do the same. We've categorized them according to the Six Seconds EQ Model.

Know Yourself

These tools increase self-awareness.

Feeling Matrix – To Enhance Emotional Literacy, this tool helps to identify the multiple feelings we have at a given time, which makes it easier to understand the messages.

Create a 3x3 grid with 9 squares. Fill in each square except the middle with a symbol, squiggle, or color representing one of the feelings you have now. Convey intensity through the intensity with which you create the lines, draw a mild feeling with light pressure and a strong feeling with strong pressure. Attempt to fill in all 8 "perimeter" squares; if necessary you can repeat a feeling.

Now look at your grid overall. How intense are the feelings overall? Which feelings are most intense? What is the range of feelings you see? Are there any unexpected feelings?

In the center box, label this mood; ideally use one or more of the basic emotions (see Emotional Literacy, above). Now that you have identified feelings, consider them: What is the message? How are these feelings trying to help you with your current situation?

Feeling Log – This tool is effective for tracking feelings over time and can be used to Recognize Patterns. It is described in more detail in *At the Heart of Leadership*.

Draw a 2x2 grid; the vertical axis is INTENSITY, the horizontal axis is PLEASANTNESS. Now you have 4 quadrants:

I - Upper Left: Intense, Unpleasant (e.g., rage, shame, grief)

II - Lower Left: Mild, Unpleasant (e.g., frustrated, bored, disappointed)

III - Lower Right: Mild, Pleasant (e.g., calm, open, patient)

IV - Upper Right: Intense, Pleasant (e.g., joyful, delighted, thrilled)

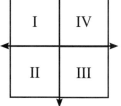

At any point, perhaps a few times a day, make a mark on the chart representing your current mood. If you like, you can put the date and time. Over the course of a week you may begin to see a pattern emerging. Consider:

- Where are you most of the time?

- Are you utilizing the full range?

- What's typically prompting you to go into each quadrant? Can you identify a "default" pattern of reaction you have been following?

- How are you moving between quadrants?

This tool can effectively be used with a group, for example to check-in on current feelings in the room before or during a discussion.

David Caruso, who partners with John Mayer and Peter Salovey, the pioneering scientists who created the concept of emotional intelligence, created an online tool for tracking moods using this matrix; you can create a free account and then use it over time. We've put a link to his tool on www.insidechange.net.

Choose Yourself

These tools develop self-management.

Ripples – This tool assists you in thinking through the consequences of a decision.

Think about a decision or choice you're considering. You can also use this to reflect on something that happened recently, such as a reaction you had.

Make a 4x4 grid. As shown in the picture, consider the impact of your choice in 4 dimensions:

- How will it help or benefit me (tactically & emotionally)

- How will it hurt or cost me (tactically & emotionally)

Me +	Others +
Me -	Others -

- How will it help or benefit others
  (tactically & emotionally)

- How will it hurt or cost others
  (tactically & emotionally)

Finally consider: What is the long-term impact of the plus side? What is the long-term impact of the minus side?

Going through this process you're using the EQ competency of Apply Consequential Thinking, which is about blending thinking and feeling to assess your choices. The tool should help you clarify whether a decision is effective – if the "plus" outweighs the "minus" then it's probably a viable choice.

You can take this model to the next level by weighting each point you write because some may have more significance than others.

VET – This is a process for Navigating Emotions, understanding and transforming them.   To use VET, you need a few minutes for quiet self-reflection – you can write or draw to help you with the process.

V: Validate – The goal is to validate – honor – the feeling. When you've succeeded at Validate you will feel the intensity of the feeling drop a little.

- Ask yourself: what are you feeling?

- Acknowledge (recognize) it.

- Name it (what is this feeling called?).

- Accept it (this is real, valid, and it's there for a reason).

E: Explore – Use your curiosity to consider the wisdom of the feelings. When you've succeeded at Explore you will have new insight.

- What is this feeling telling me? What's the message?

- What is this protecting or serving? What is it pushing me to pay attention to?

- What does this feeling push or pull me to do?

- What happened before, and what might happen after?

- What great advice does this feeling offer?

T: Transform – Shift your focus to another useful feeling and "lean in" to strengthen it, moving yourself to a new emotional state. When you've succeeded at Transform you will feel a new feeling.

Consider: What do I want to be feeling now? Do I have any of that feeling? If not, what other feelings do I have at the moment that I can VET?

Focus on the new feeling, strengthening it.

Once you've done the V and the E effectively, the T will be relatively easy – if you're "working too hard," go back to step 1.

You can use VET with yourself or with another person. The VET process takes a little practice. It's especially difficult, and powerful, when you're frustrated.

Hope with a Plan - This tool will help you consider an optimistic perspective on a struggle, problem, or failure. We call optimism "hope with a plan." The benefit is increased problem-solving ability and energy to move forward.

First, think about the problem in a highly pessimistic view; complete each sentence:

- Time: This will last forever because…

- Isolation: This will ruin everything because…

- Effort: There is absolutely nothing I can do about it because…

Now, challenge those assertions. What is something about each statement you wrote that is not true? Write a new, realistic, balanced assertion about the problem in terms of:

- Time (how long will this last?)

- Isolation (how much will this affect?)

- Effort (what is possible now?)

Again, this tool can be used by yourself or with others, and is particularly effective if you practice it over time. The basic principal is what Optimism researcher Martin Seligman calls "Disputing," which is the skill of challenging the internal voice of pessimism.

Fueling the Fire – This is a tool for increasing intrinsic motivation. This will increase your lasting energy.

- If you had the capability right now, what are three things you would stop?

- For each one, what would you start instead?

- Which of your core values would be supported and nurtured if you started these things?

What is one of the three things that you could step towards in the project or plan you're working on this week? What would that step look like if it were truly successful?

Give Yourself

These tools will create greater self-direction, connecting you with others and with purpose.

Compassionate Curiosity – Empathy is a powerful tool for understanding and connecting with others. One way to access empathy is through curiosity.

Consider someone with whom you are not connecting, or with whom you feel a bit disconnected (but want to be connected).

Think of a situation you were both in. Make a chart with two columns, one for you, one for them.

- How do you see what happened (the facts)?

- If you were the other person, how would you see what happened (the facts)?

- How do you see the feelings?

- If you were the other person, how would you see the feelings?

Look at your chart so far. What does it tell you about your feelings toward the other person? How compassionately have you portrayed them? If you saw this person as truly good (but perhaps making some mistakes), would you change any of your chart? Do so.

How do you see the person now?

Your Billboard – The EQ competency of Pursue Noble Goals is about putting your purpose into action. When you do so, you become much more powerful – able to manage your own reactions at a profound level, and also able to galvanize others.

Sometimes airports and other public places give advertising space to pro-social causes. Imagine that you had the opportunity to put a message out that a million people would see next week.

Draw and write the design of the billboard.

Consider:

- How would this change people who saw it?

- How would that change help people?

- How would that change help you?

- What is truly important to you about that change?

- What is one way you can model or act out that change yourself, in a small way, tomorrow?

More Resources

There are many good books to help you continue to develop emotional intelligence. Please see www.insidechange.net for recommendations, here are several:

The Leader as a Mensch by Bruna Martinuzzi – an inspiring book of reflections and practical tips for leaders to be real human beings.

The EQ Action Log by Mimi Frenette – a reflection tool for setting and pursuing your goals.

At the Heart of Leadership by Joshua Freedman – a practical book about the Six Seconds EQ Model applied to leadership.

Emotions Revealed by Paul Ekman – a rich scientific exploration of emotions and facial expression.

The Emotionally Intelligent Manager by David Caruso and Peter Salovey – a solid introduction to a scientific model of emotional intelligence with implications for management.

True North by Bill George and Peter Sims – a call to leaders to identify purpose.

Crucial Conversations by Kerry Patterson, Joseph Grenny, Ron McMillan, Al Switzler – a framework for increasing compassionate honesty in addressing difficult issues.

Recap

Remember, your emotional state will strongly influence the way others react to you. They'll automatically move into resistance if you come on with a perceived attack. Conversely they'll get bored and disengage if you come on too soft. Worst of all, if you are inauthentic, you will lose trust. So you can't "play at it," you've actually got to transform yourself to be the necessary emotional catalyst for the change process.

 Change starts on the inside.

Nearly all men can stand adversity,
but if you want to test a man's character,
give him power.

– Abraham Lincoln

Chapter 8: Power

There is extensive research on the role of power in change. We'll explore this in terms of the use of power to facilitate change, and in terms of the effect of power on you as an agent of change.

Two professors from the University of Amsterdam wrote a synthesis of the research to date, outlining five different models of power and the type of change the flows from that view of power.[74] Their definitions are excerpted below. As you look at the different models, consider two questions:

Which is closest to your vision of power?

Which is the method of change that best fits your needs?

Position Power, Domination and the Power Model of Change

Power: The use of power requires that you control or possess relevant power sources in order to get another person to do what you want.

Change: The leader is an authority figure who imposes and declares organizational change, and pushes the change by mandate.

Personal Power, Influence, and the Expert Model of Change

Power: The emphasis is on power sources connected to particular abilities, skills, and experience of an actor (through competence, relationships, reputation, group support, control over resources and knowledge and information, charisma).

Change: Change agents use expert knowledge to assist groups in the organization with analyzing and solving problems.

Structural Power, Exchange, and the Negotiation Model of Change

Power: Organizational processes are influenced both by mutual harmonization of parts of the system, and by the way power is structured and used.

Change: The change managers focus on preventing conflict in the change process by regulating participation of the groups involved, by top-down decision making and implementation, or by negotiation about the objectives of the change process and the way it is organized and managed.

Cultural Power, Management of Meaning and the Sales Model of Change

Power: Culture represents relative stability in an organization and is related to power because the power relations are seen as natural and unquestionable. Perceptions, cognitions, and preferences of individuals and groups are shaped by culture that prevents them from seeing alternatives.

Change: In the process of change constituents "sell" their visions, and over time there arises commitment, adoption of the new organizational constellation, and a harmonious development of new meaning.

Power Dynamics, Dialogue, and the Developmental Model of Change

Power: Rather than a set "base" of power, this model considers that everyone in an organization has power, internal, through relationships, and through their capacity to influence.

Change: Through open dialogue, participants develop an understanding of each other's perspectives, interests, and convictions as a prerequisite for developing a common image of a desirable future. Change comes through organizational learning and participation.

Each of the models that Boonstra and Bennebroeck present has a valid application; it's not that one type of power is "right." Presumably all of these exist, and to some degree you, as a change leader, could exercise any or all. So two considerations: To what degree is each available to you?

And perhaps the most important consideration: What are the costs and benefits of each? For example, a benefit of "Positional Power" is that it can drive a fast result. A benefit of "Dynamic Power" is that it is self-reinforcing.

So consider that for a moment – here's a chart for you to use for self-reflection:

Type of Power (and way to use it)	Costs of Using This	Benefits of Using This
Positional Power (domination)		
Personal Power (influence)		
Structural Power (negotiation)		
Cultural Power (selling ideas)		
Dynamic Power (dialogue)		

We can pretty it up, use different words that are more "politically correct," but we can't change the fact: As a change leader, you are exercising power.

So where are you getting the power, and what are you doing with it? With power comes risk - the price can be very high, and the results can be horrific. On the other hand, scary or not, you have power. There are only three options we know of:

Use it with accountability and profound respect.

Abuse it to fuel your own pride.

Deny it and be a victim.

By the way, it's easy to say "well #1 is the right answer," but the brutal truth is that we all do #2 and #3 at times. The question isn't "Which is right," but "How do I made #1 fully alive for me and for those whose lives I touch?"

So it's important to notice when you're slipping into the role of dictator or victim, versus when you're maintaining your power as an ally, coach, and true leader. It's a kind of "teeter totter;" you can get out of balance toward dictator or toward victim; the accountable stance is poised in the middle. Reflect on this. Notice the internal and external conditions that tip you one way or another. What will it take for you to strengthen your ability to stay balanced on the fulcrum?

The task of leadership
is not to put greatness into people
but to elicit it,
for the greatness is there already.

– John Buchan

Chapter 9:
You as a Change Leader

As you wrap up the book, we want you to reconsider the basics of motivation. We've said that change will only work if people are deeply engaged, and that drive comes from within. So we'll revisit the subject of internal motivation.

Then, to conclude, we'd like you to consider yourself in this process. Are you a leader? Are you a change leader? What's your vision of yourself as someone involved in change?

Internal Motivation[75]

People are paid to do their work, and eventually should lose their jobs if they don't meet expectations. But in most roles, in most organizations, star performance requires a higher level of engagement – a commitment that goes beyond the paycheck. That extra commitment is called "discretionary effort" because it's at the employee's discretion. He gives that extra because he wants to – because he feels like it. True leaders are able to inspire that feeling.

As FedEx founder Fred Smith said, "Leadership is getting people to work for you when they are not obligated."

As we consider "motivating employees" we can divide the work we want to achieve into two basic categories of outcomes. One category is for those basic, task-oriented, behavioral pieces of work. Showing up on time. Filing required reports. Making the required number of calls. They tend to be prescribed, tactical, and easily measurable.

Rather than clear tasks, the other category is about the **way** employees work. We want them to care for customers. To innovate new solutions. To inspire commitment. To trust and be trustworthy.

An iceberg is a useful metaphor for these two categories. At the tip of the iceberg are those visible, tangible activities. Beneath the surface are the invisible, emotional drivers which shape attitude. These emotional drivers make the difference in **how** activities are done and thereby define the impact employees have on customers and colleagues. Above the surface is what's visible. Below is what's invisible. Above is BEHAVIOR, below is what DRIVES behavior.

In addition to different categories of outcomes, there are different kinds of motivators; different "levers" that managers can use to strengthen performance. There are two basic categories for these levers: "extrinsic" and "intrinsic":

Extrinsic motivators	Intrinsic motivators
Live outside the employee (e.g., bonuses, perks, fines, employee of the month).	Live inside the employee (e.g., passion, alignment with values, belonging, purpose).
Delivered by the manager or the organization.	Driven by relationships and organizational climate.
Easy to quantify, concrete.	Intangible, abstract.
Require ongoing expense (e.g., more bonus funds).	Self-maintaining and spread from employee to employee.
Reinforce power structure (manager decides).	Reinforce interdependence (shared responsibility).

While we can categorize two kinds of motivators, it's more accurate to consider a spectrum. For example, while salary is extrinsic, many employees are using their salary to support their families, which can be intrinsic.

Not surprisingly, different kinds of motivators drive different kinds of performance. But one of the most dangerous and common pitfalls in organizations is the use of one type of motivator for all employees and all goals.

Take a typical incentive program where salespeople get a bonus for meeting a quota. The salesperson is rewarded for making the sale irrespective of **how** it's done. Many salespeople like it and it's easy for sales managers. However, the operations people are rarely thrilled with the way salespeople over-promise to customers. Or, what happens when the business changes and salespeople need to collaborate?

We're starting to see some of the complexities of motivation, and how different factors motivate people in different situations. One of the keys to this puzzle is to match different types of motivators that will drive different types of needs.

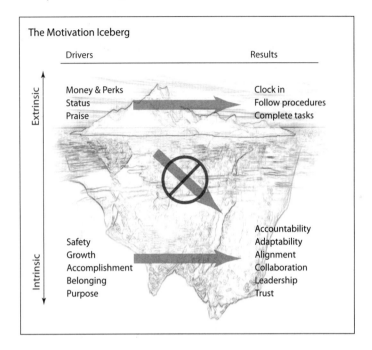

In the Motivation Iceberg graphic, you can see that on the left are two categories of drivers and on the right are two categories of results.

- The **extrinsic** ("above the surface") motivators drive "above the surface" outcomes.

- The **intrinsic** ("below the waterline") motivators drive "below the surface" outcomes.

What's critical to remember is that extrinsic levers (top left) do not effectively motivate the deeper results (bottom right). In fact, emphasizing these extrinsic influences can undermine the deeper "beneath the surface" commitment.

This is not to say the extrinsic motivators are irrelevant, but rather to say we need to use the correct motivator for the desired outcome.

The big challenge is that because it is incredibly easy to offer an extrinsic carrot or stick, that method is the default. Extrinsic factors are measurable, concrete, and reinforce the power structure in the organization – which makes these quite attractive to organizational systems. Quite satisfying except for one key obstacle: when it comes to engaging hearts and minds, **they don't work.***

Three tips for engaging intrinsic motivation:

While it's more work to develop intrinsic motivators, if you want to engage those "beneath the waterline" outcomes, this work is not optional. Here are three tips:

1. Develop a culture of trust.

Are your employees free to express their thoughts? Are they feeling safe enough to disagree with you? Can they challenge all the existing assumptions? Creating a culture of acceptance of the diverse views is the key to boost the potential of people and to increase trust. Two other "must haves" for trust are consistency (people know what to expect, leaders walk the talk), and caring (people know that while leaders are responsible to the business, they also genuinely care about the individuals).

---

*   For an excellent review of the evidence of this assertion, see *DRIVE* by Daniel Pink and our interview with Pink on www.6seconds.org. For more discussion of intrinsic versus extrinsic motivation, Alfie Kohn's book, *Unconditional Parenting*, is quite intriguing (though obviously not a business book, it has applications for all of us).

2. Connect with people.

One of the, or perhaps THE, fundamental intrinsic motivator is belonging. Humans are pack animals, and as such we are wired to connect. Yet most senior leaders have a double- and triple-booked schedule filled months ahead with nearly no opportunity to interact on a human level.

When was the last time you were "just hanging out" at lunch with team members two or three levels below you? When was the last truly honest conversation you had with a colleague in which you genuinely listened to her story? How much time are you spending connecting with people outside your team and business unit versus inside? This is not rocket science, but it is just as powerful.

3. Constantly articulate purpose.

Why does your organization exist? It makes money in order to exist, but what does it exist for? If you don't have a compelling, powerful answer to that question you will not build enduring intrinsic motivation, and the best people will not stay with you – so get a great consultant/coach and develop an answer.

If you do have that answer, an answer that is worth fighting for, then tell that story over and over. Stand up for it, and make sure it stands out. Everything you do should serve that purpose, and if it doesn't, change what you do. Every change you make, every message you roll out, should be linked to that purpose. Junior employees will rarely say it out loud, but just know they're constantly asking, "Why should I give you my all?" Make sure you've got a worthwhile answer, and then make sure they hear it.

While this work is challenging, it has long-lasting benefits. When you get these core drivers in place they become part of the organizational culture. Intrinsic motivation lasts. But who has time?

Discussing this type of work with leaders, many of our clients' first reactions is: "This sounds right, but I just don't have time." If you're like most managers, you have too much to do just getting the basic tasks completed. It's like you're on a treadmill chasing to catch up. So here's a hard truth: Unless you do the leadership work of building intrinsic motivation, your treadmill is just going to go faster and faster.

There is no "right time" to stop chasing and start leading. No one is going to gift you with blocks of uninterrupted time to shift your attention to the "heart of the iceberg." Yet that's where the real opportunity lives.

Starting in the mid 1980s, James Kouzes and Barry Posner began surveying business people all around the world asking, "What do you look for and admire in a leader?" In essence, the answer is *the capability to envision a worthwhile future then support and enable others to pursue that.* The terrible news is that only 3% of a leaders' time is dedicated to this activity.[76] And pay attention: They found it is not enough to have a vision, rather a *shared vision* where people genuinely feel part of it! As we've discussed, real vision is not a static idea on a plaque, it's a living process. If we're going to be successful with change, we need to go far beyond 3% of the time, and we need to do it right.

The ultimate measure of a man

is not where he stands

in moments of comfort,

but where he stands

at times of challenge and controversy.

- Martin Luther King, Jr.

A Leader Worth Following[77]

To conclude this book, let us ask you again this question: What is your purpose?

We've talked about the phases of change spinning like a wheel. We've said we want you to be able to accelerate this process and that you'll develop a lot of human energy, unleash a lot power, in the process. So the axel has to be strong! The axel is purpose. The wheel won't go anywhere without it.

 So what's your purpose? What's the organization's purpose? And are you sure the change you're driving moves you closer to it?

A few years ago we enjoyed a business climate where companies flourished with little effort; stocks soared, cash was everywhere, and growth seemed automatic. Now we're in a dramatically different realm.

What does it take to lead today? Not just to "muddle along," but to truly lead? To take people and organizations to heights they would not otherwise reach, to be someone worth following?

The turbulent times in which we are living can create pressure, stress, fear and so on, but they also offer an extraordinary opportunity for true leaders to emerge. Anyone with a pulse can grow when times are flush, not so when times are lean.

What does it take? In keynotes and consulting projects, we frequently ask groups to tell us. We ask them to think of a leader who inspired them to go above and beyond – a leader who helped them become and do more than they thought possible.

In the last years we've asked this of widely eclectic groups in over a dozen countries: from aerospace engineers to finance executives, from preschool teachers to pharmaceutical scientists, from manufacturing factory workers to luxury hotel managers. Perhaps it won't be a surprise that their answers were quite similar.

Before we share their answers, please take a moment to consider the question for yourself:

- Think of a leader who helped bring out your very best. Someone you consider "a leader worth following."

- What did you feel with this person?

- What did s/he do to inspire this?

While the answers vary somewhat, there's a fairly consistent story. Leaders worth following inspire us, they help us feel a rare mix of challenge and excitement, passion and guts, willingness to sweat along with a heady joie de vivre.

What do these exceptional leaders do?

- Listen / Give me time

- Encourage / Challenge / Give me feedback (critical as well as praising)

- Take risks on me / Give me a chance

- Express their passion / Live their vision

It's absolutely critical to note: These behaviors alone are not enough. **There is a "secret sauce" or "x-factor" that sets these people apart, and that's the WAY they do what they do.** Based in genuine care, they take these actions authentically, naturally, and consistently. Not only do they walk their talk, they also talk their walk.

True leaders offer a match between who they are, what they do, and the way they do it. We can take any action in multiple ways – when we take the right action, in the right way, and for the right reasons we get the most power. The mass of the shaft lines up behind the point of the arrow.

According to the groups we've surveyed, when leaders accomplish this alignment, they engender key reactions, including trust, commitment, and a passion for excellence. They help people feel both safe and "on fire" – perhaps it's only from a foundation of real safety that people can take the extraordinary risks to excel?

As "times get tougher" and change challenges accelerate, the skills of emotional intelligence become even more critical for true leaders. As stress and anxiety increase, people become more reactive, more survival-oriented, and less innovative. So in times like these, true leaders provide both comfort and challenge. They help people channel the general unease and take action to make a difference. They keep a vision of possibility without denying the pain of the present. They take risks in spite of, maybe even because of, the prevalent fear. They blend head and heart to be trustworthy, courageous, and authentic – to take care of their people and walk together toward a compelling purpose.

Then when the dust settles – as it always does – those leaders have taken their people head and shoulders above the competition.

So consider:

- Are you a leader worth following?

- Are you taking your people someplace worth going?

- And, what skills do you need to "tune up," to stand out as a leader in times of change?

In these changing times, whether you are in a formal leader-ship role or not, you have a choice about how you are showing up and using your influence and personal power. As a change leader, you are going someplace and asking others to come along. Is it to a place worth going?

A ship in harbor is safe –

but that is not what ships are for.

– John A. Shedd

End Notes

1 | "The Enterprise of the Future: IBM Global CEO Study 2008." IBM Corporation. May 2008. www.ibm.com/enterpriseofthefuture

2 | Freedman, Joshua (2010). 2010 Workplace Issues Report, http://www.6seconds.org/blog/2010/02/talent-performance-economy/. Freedman, Joshua (2007): 2007 Workplace Issues Report, http://www.6seconds.org/blog/2007/12/2007-workplace-issues-report/

3 | Burke, Lisa (2010). A Missing Link in the Transfer Problem? Understanding How Trainers Learn About Training Transfer. *Human Resource Management* (in press)

4 | Borsato, Larry (2008). Information Overload on the Web, and Searching for the Right Sifting Tool. http://www.the-standard.com/news/2008/08/28/knowledge-doubling-curve

5 | Gonzalez, Cathy (2004). The Role of Blended Learning in the World of Technology. Benchmarks Online. http://www.unt.edu/benchmarks/archives/2004/september04/eis.htm

6 | IBM Global Technology Services (2006). The Toxic Terabyte: How Data-Dumping Threatens Business Efficiency. IBM United Kingdom Limited

7 | More on this in Freedman, Joshua (2007): A Hope for Change: Alan Deutschman on Change or Die. www.6seconds.org

8 | Bovey, WH, & Hede, A. (2001). Resistance to Organizational Change: The Role of Cognitive and Affective Processes. *Leadership & Organization Development Journal, 22*(8), 372 - 382

9 | Devos, Geert; Vanderheyden, Karlien; Van Den Broeck, Herman (2002). A Framework for Assessing Commitment to Change. *Process and Context Variables of Organizational Change.* Vlerick Working Papers

10 | Freedman, J (2008). The Business Case for Emotional Intelligence. www.6seconds.org/case

11 | Fariselli, L, et al (2009). Stress, Emotional Intelligence, and Performance in Healthcare. www.6seconds.org

12 | Bovey, Wayne H., Hede, Andrew, 2001, Resistance to Organisational Change: the Role of Defence Mechanisms. *Journal of Managerial Psychology*, 16, 534-548

13 | Hurley Robert (2006). Decision to Trust, *Harvard Business Review*, September

14 | Freedman, Joshua (2007): A Hope for Change: Alan Deutschman on Change or Die. www.6seconds.org

15 | The concept of action learning was first documented in the 1940s by physicist Reginald Revans who trained UK hospital teams to reflect on their actions and ask good questions to improve their processes

16 | Bridges, William (2009). *Managing Transitions: Making the Most of Change* (third edition). Da Capo Lifelong Books

17 | Thank you to Allen Zingg for this important point about resistance going underground

18 | The Gore example comes from Alan Deutschman in Freedman, Joshua (2007): A Hope for Change: Alan Deutschman on Change or Die. www.6seconds.org

19 | Garlick, D. (2003). Integrating Brain Science Research with Intelligence Research. *Psychological Science*, 12(5), 185-188

20 | *ibid*

21 | Adapted from *The Brain Fitness Program*. PBS Video

22 | Raichle ME (1998). The Neural Correlates of Consciousness: An Analysis of Cognitive Skill Learning. *Phil Trans R Soc Lond* B 353:1889–901

23 | Phelps, E.A., & LeDoux, J. (2005). Contributions of the Amygdala to Emotion Processing: From Animal Models to Human Behavior. *Neuron* 48:175-87

24 | Pally, R. (2007). The Predicting Brain: Unconscious Repetition, Conscious Reflection and Therapeutic Change. *International Journal of Psychoanalysis*, 88, 861-881 (p. 862)

25 | Phelps, E.A., & LeDoux, J. (2005). Contributions of the Amygdala to Emotion Processing: From Animal Models to Human Behavior. *Neuron* 48:175-87

26 | Nadel, L. & Land C. (2000). Memory Traces Revisited. *National Review of Neuroscience*, 1, 209-212

27 | Treasure, J., Tchanturia, K., & Schmidt, U. (2005). Developing a Model of the Treatment for Eating Disorder: Using Neuroscience Research to Examine the How Rather than the What of Change. *Counseling and Psychotherapy Research*, 5(3), 191-202

28 | Weissman, D.H., Roberts, K.C., Visscher, K.M., Woldorff, M. G. (2006). The Neural Bases of Momentary Lapses in Attention. *Nature Neuroscience*, 9 (7), 971-978.

29 | Pally, R. (2007). The Predicting Brain: Unconscious Repetition, Conscious Reflection and Therapeutic Change. *International Journal of Psychoanalysis*, 88, 861-881. (p. 872)

30 | Iacoboni M, Molnar-Szakacs I, Gallese V, Buccino G, Mazziot-

ta JC (2005). Grasping the Intentions of Others with One's Own Mirror-neuron System. *PLoS Biol* 3:e79

31 | Cole, M., Cole, S.R., & Lightfoot, C. (2005). *The Development of Children* (5th ed). New York: Worth Publishers

32 | Gallese, V. (n.d.). Intentional Attunement: The Mirror Neuron System and its Role in Interpersonal Relations. *European Science Foundation*. Retrieved January 30, 2007 from http://www.inter-disciplines.org/mirror/papers/1

33 | Rizzolatti, G. & Craighero, L. (2004). The Mirror-neuron System. *Annual Review of Neuroscience*, 27. 169-192.

34 | Gallese, V. (2006). Intentional Attunement: A Neuropsychological Perspective on Social Cognition and its Disruption in Autism. *Brain Research*, 1079. 15-24
Goldman, A.I., & Sekhar Sripada, C. (2003). Simulationalist Models of Face-based Emotion Recognition. *Cognition*, 94, 193-213

35 | Gazzola, V., Aziz-Zadeh, L., & Keysers, C. (2006). Empathy and the Somatotopic Auditory Mirror System in Humans. *Current Biology*, 16. 1824-1829

36 | *ibid*

37 | Gallese, V. (2006). Intentional Attunement: A Neuropsychological Perspective on Social Cognition and its Disruption in Autism. *Brain Research*, 1079. 15-24 and
Neumann, R., & Strack, F. (2000). "Mood contagion": The Automatic Transfer of Mood Between Persons. *Journal of Personality and Social Psychology*, 79 (2), 211-223

38 | Neumann, R., & Strack, F. (2000). "Mood Contagion": The Automatic Transfer of Mood Between Persons. *Journal of Personality and Social Psychology*, 79 (2), 211-223

39 | Gallese, V. (2006). Intentional Attunement: A Neuropsychological Perspective on Social Cognition and its Disruption in Au-

tism. *Brain Research*, 1079. 15-24

40 | Bandura, A. (2002). Reflexive Empathy: On Predicting More Than has Ever Been Observed. *Behavioral and Brain Sciences*, 25, 24-25

41 | Barsade, S.G. (2002). The Ripple Effect: Emotional Contagion and its Influence on Group Behavior. *Administrative Science Quarterly*, 47 (4), 644-675

42 | Sy, Côté, & Saavedra, 2005, as cited in Barsade, S.G., & Gibson, D.E. (2007). Why Does Affect Matter in Organizations? *Academy of Management Perspectives*, 36-59

43 | Isen, A. (1993). Positive Affect and Decision Making. In M. Lewis & J.M. Haviland (Eds.), *The Handbook of Emotion* (pp 261-277). New York: The Guliford Press

44 | Elsbach, K., & Barr, P. (1999). Effects of Mood on Individuals' Use of Structure Decision Protocols. *Organization Science*, 10 (2), 181-198

45 | Hong, Kessely, and Iris Bohnet (2007). Status and Distrust: The Relevance of Inequality and Betrayal Aversion. *Journal of Economic Psychology*, 28, 197–213

46 | Naef, Michael, Ernst Fehr, Urs Fischbacher, Jürgen Schupp, and Gert Wagner (2008). Decomposing Trust: Explaining National and Ethnical Trust Differences. Working paper, Institute for Empirical Research in Economics, University of Zurich

47 | Adolphs Ralph, 2002, Trust in the Brain. *Nature Neuroscience* 5, 192–193

48 | Kosfeld, Michael, Markus Heinrichs, Paul J. Zak, Urs Fischbacher, and Ernst Fehr (2005). Oxytocin Increases Trust in Humans. *Nature*, 435, 673–676

49 | Bohnet, Iris, Bruno S. Frey, and Steffen Huck (2001). More Order with Less Law: On Contract Enforcement, Trust, and

Crowding. *American Political Science Review*, 95, 131–144

Fehr, Ernst, and Armin Falk (2002). Psychological Foundations of Incentives. *European Economic Review*, 46, 687–724

Falk, Armin, and Kosfeld, Michael (2006). The Hidden Costs of Control. *American Economic Review*, 96, 1611–1630

50 | Zak, P. J., Kurzban, R., & Matzner, W. T. (2005). Oxytocin is Associated with Human Trustworthiness. *Hormones and Behavior*, 48, 522-527

51 | Zak, Paul J., 2005, The Neuroeconomics of Trust. Claremont Graduate University - Center for Neuroeconomics Studies Working paper

52 | Baumgartner, Thomas, Markus Heinrichs, Aline Vonlanthen, Urs Fischbacher, and Ernst Fehr (2008). Oxytocin Shapes the Neural Circuitry of Trust and Trust Adaptation in Humans. *Neuron*, 58, 639–650

53 | Fehr, Ernst, and Armin Falk (2002). Psychological Foundations of Incentives. *European Economic Review*, 46, 687–724

54 | Thank you to Mimi Frenette, one of Six Seconds' coaches, for this powerful tool!

55 | For more about Navigating Emotions, see "The Wisdom of Feelings" chapter in *At the Heart of Leadership* by Joshua Freedman

56 | Shunryu Suzuki (2006), *Zen Mind, Beginner's Mind*. Shambhala

57 | Hannah, S., Sweeney, P. & Lester, P. (2007). Toward a Courageous Mindset: The Subjective Act and Experience of Courage. *The Journal of Positive Psychology: Dedicated to furthering research and promoting good practice*, 2(2), 129-135. Also see this blog post from Jeremy Dean's intriguing blog: http://www.spring.org.uk/2007/08/how-to-build-courage-through.php

58 | Pally, R. (2007). The Predicting Brain: Unconscious Repetition, Conscious Reflection and Therapeutic Change. *International Journal of Psychoanalysis*, 88, 861-881

59 | Burke, Lisa (2010). A Missing link in the Transfer Problem? Understanding How Trainers Learn About Training Transfer. *Human Resource Management* (in press)

60 | Freedman, Joshua (2007): A Hope for Change: Alan Deutschman on Change or Die. www.6seconds.org

61 | Adapted from Vroom Victor (1964). *Work and Motivation*. New York: Wiley

62 | Ekman, Paul. (2007). *Emotions Revealed*. Macmillan

63 | For more on this model of optimism, see Martin Seligman's book, *Learned Optimism*, or take the SEI Assessment

64 | Collins, James (2001). *Good to Great: Why Some Companies Make the Leap... and Others Don't*. HarperBusiness

65 | Lieberman, Matthew D et al (2007) Putting Feelings Into Words: Affect Labeling Disrupts Amygdala Activity in Response to Affective Stimuli. *Psychological Science*, Vol. 18, Issue 5, Page 421

66 | Freedman, Joshua (2007). *At the Heart of Leadership: How to Get Results With Emotional Intelligence*. Six Seconds

67 | WordNet: http://wordnetweb.princeton.edu/perl/webwn?s=judgement

68 | Kang MJ, et al (2009). The Wick in the Candle of Learning: Epistemic Curiosity Activates Reward Circuitry and Enhances Memory. *Psychol Sci*. 2009 Aug;20(8):963-73

69 | Fast, N. J., & Tiedens, L. Z. (2010). Blame Contagion: The Automatic Transmission of Self-serving Attributions. *Journal of Experimental Social Psychology*, 46, 97-106

70 | Kelly, Tom (2001). *The Art of Innovation: Lessons in Creativity from IDEO, America's Leading Design Firm*. Broadway Business

71 | Joshua Freedman, Massimiliano Ghini and Carina Fiedeldey-Van Dijk (2006). Emotional Intelligence and Performance, www.6seconds.org/sei - Six Seconds

72 | Freedman, Joshua (2007). *At the Heart of Leadership: How to Get Results with Emotional Intelligence*. Six Seconds

73 | Freedman, J., Ghini, M., Jensen, A. (2005). *Six Seconds Emotional Intelligence Assessment*, Six Seconds (www.6seconds.org/sei)

74 | Boonstra, J.J., & Bennebroeck Gravenhorst, K.M. 1998. Power dynamics and organizational change. A comparison of perspectives. *European Journal of Work and Organizational Psychology*, 7: 97-120

75 | This section is adapted from one of our training curricula: Freedman, J. and Kniveton, K. (2009). "Motivation from the Inside Out," *Developing Human Performance*. Six Seconds (www.6seconds.org/dhp)

76 | Kouzes, James, and Posner, Barry (2008). *The Leadership Challenge*, 4th edition. Jossey-Bass

77 | This section is adapted from: Freedman, J (2009): Being a Leader Worth Following. Six Seconds (www.6seconds.org)

Indexed Contents

Part I

Part II

Part III

Truth always originates

in a minority of one,

and every custom begins

as a broken precedent.

– William J. Durant

Acknowledgements

We've learned about change working with incredible client-partners. Thank you for your trust in us and for letting us be part of your change journey.

We are grateful to our team for their incredible commitment to creating positive change, starting from the inside.

Anabel Jensen has been our "guiding light" in maintaining a commitment to look at the inside. Todd Everett was one of the co-creators of our original EQ Change Model. Tom Wojick helped us apply and refine the model in practical ways.

Lorenzo Fariselli has been an incredible partner in developing tools to measure what matters; along with Federica Valentina who keeps the tools running smoothly, and Carina Fiedeldey-Van Dijk who raises the bar.

The team at Incite Partners have been allies in clarifying our message and communication of our brand and promise. Thank you to Dan Caine, John Burgess, and Mark Lee. And for the cover of this book!

We'd also like to thank our other team members in the Italy office, Daniela di Ciaccio, and Veruscka Gennari – and in the US, Marsha Rideout, Yoshimi Miyazaki, Jenny Wiley, Marilynn Jorgensen, Alex Russell, Jay Grant and Debbie Havert, for putting EQ in action, and, to Karen McCown for the vision. You're true difference-makers.

Finally, **mille grazie to Patty and Sabri,** we couldn't do this without you.

About the Authors

Joshua Freedman is one of the world's leading specialists on developing and applying emotional intelligence to improve performance. A leader, author, and educator, Freedman takes hard science and makes it applicable. He specializes in building custom solutions for organizations seeking to integrate EQ with measurable ROI.

For over a decade he has helped lead the world's preeminent emotional intelligence organization, developing offices in six countries; top practitioners and researchers; renown scientists and leaders as advisory board members; and award-winning materials including five validated assessment tools.

Joshua is the author of *At the Heart of Leadership*, a practical guide for leaders to tap the power of emotions to get better results, as well as numerous assessment and development tools to improve the people-side of performance.

Massimiliano Ghini, MBA, is the President of Six Seconds Italia. A professor of Human Resources Management and People Management at Alma Graduate School (AGS), the Business School of the University of Bologna. At AGS Max is in charge of Organization and Personnel of the Executive MBA.

Max is also a consultant for organizational development and change management in large and medium companies; he has a proven track-record of emotional intelligence training and consulting since 1999.

Max is the coauthor and project leader of the Six Seconds Emotional Intelligence Assessment (SEI), and the author of several articles and white paper on EQ in Italian. His research, articles and findings were published on Fortune, Ilsole24ore, Direzione del Personale.

From the Publisher

Six Seconds is a global organization supporting people to harness the power and wisdom of feelings to make a positive difference - everywhere, all the time.

Utilizing powerful models and tools based in current neuroscience, Six Seconds' consultants and trainers are people-experts supporting businesses, government agencies, nonprofits, schools, and families to thrive. Six Seconds is a global network with offices in six countries and certified practitioners in over 100 nations, all committed to being change leaders – starting from the inside.

Learn more about Six Seconds online:

www.6seconds.org

To see Six Seconds' other publications:

www.6seconds.org/tools

Inside Change In Action

The INSIDE CHANGE CERTIFICATION PROGRAM supports leaders to be more effective on the people-side of performance.

Designed in alignment with the principles of this book, this isn't just a training – it's a blended program combining metrics, learning, coaching and support for success.

For information about the program, to reach to authors, and learn more about INSIDE CHANGE, see:

www.insidechange.net